THE MEANING OF HOME

The Meaning of Home

Edwin Heathcote

FRANCES LINCOLN LIMITED
PUBLISHERS

Frances Lincoln Ltd
4 Torriano Mews
Torriano Avenue,
London NW5 2RZ
www.franceslincoln.com

The Meaning of Home
Copyright © Edwin Heathcote 2012

First Frances Lincoln edition 2012

A catalogue record for this book is available from the British Library

ISBN 978-0-7112-3377-5

Printed in China

9 8 7 6 5 4 3 2 1

CONTENTS

INTRODUCTION: HOME IS WHERE THE HEART IS

WHAT DOES A HOME MEAN? It might sound a stupid question, the very idea of home is so tied up with our *selves* that it can seem almost inseparable from our being. We fear the idea of homelessness, it means a life on the streets, of not having a place to sleep, to eat, to be. Our home is our base, a place that roots us to the earth, to the city or the landscape; it gives us permanence and stability and allows us to build a life around it and within it. When we are away from it we pine, we are homesick. We have learned to dimly despise the non-places of airports and offices, of malls and motorways, places that are everywhere and nowhere, places that are globally familiar and unnervingly similar. We yearn to return to the familiar rootedness of our sofas and our own beds, places with which we are comfortable and in which we feel we are safe.

Then again, we have also been persuaded that our homes are assets, that they are our pensions and our financial security for an uncertain future, that we ought to be part of a home-owning democracy. Our homes have been turned into political tools – it is the spectre of homelessness that keeps us working and our mortgages which chain us to our work and allow us to live in a state of insistent mild fear. A home can be an asset and it can be a burden, a place of comfort and a weight around our necks. A 'mortgage' is literally a pledge to death.

But beyond the obvious, beyond the idea of the home as a refuge and a focus for family life, what does it *mean*? Martin Heidegger proposed that the building of a house and the idea of dwelling on the earth were fundamentally connected. The German word for building, *bauen* (as in Bauhaus), and the English word *being* share the same root. The etymology survives in English only in the word 'neighbour' from the High German and Old English for 'nigh' or 'near dweller'. To *build*, it seems, is to *be*. Carl Jung similarly stressed the intimate association of the house with the self when he analysed a dream he himself had had while on a 1909 voyage to the US with Sigmund Freud. He described a dream of being in a house that was obviously 'my house' yet with which he was unfamiliar and through which he set on a journey of discovery, from its Rococo upper floors, its medieval ground floor to its dark Roman cellars. In analysing his own dream, Jung came to his hugely influential idea of a 'collective unconscious', that this house represented something that went beyond his personal experience and descended into a universal well of consciousness that pervades the minds of all mankind. The house, Jung proposed, was a model of the mind.

When the Roman orators looked for a way of organizing their knowledge and their rhetorical devices, they too looked to the house. They created 'memory palaces' in which facts were placed in rooms, given physical locations within a real and remembered or imagined house. The mind, it seems can retain huge amounts of information if it is associated with architectural locations in a house, or a palace.

The idea of the house is also deeply entwined not only with our language but in its very building blocks, the alphabet. To the Cretans, the *aleph* was an ox (turn the capital 'A' upside down and you can see a head with two horns), although in the Kabbalah tradition it is the mystical origin of everything, the number that contains all others. When Jorge Luis Borges wrote his remarkable short story 'The Aleph', however, it had transformed into a point in a cellar below the house of the useless poet Daneri, from which every other moment in time and space can be seen, an infinity compressed into a pinpoint, a singularity. The house is ultimately demolished though the suggestion is that this aleph might not be the only one. This extraordinary fiction, the idea that a cellar could contain a point of infinity, seems to reflect Jung's dream of his cellar, the archaeology of the mind.

The second component of the word alphabet, *beta*, derives directly from the word 'Beth', or house, a word which survives in Hebrew. The Cretan pictograph depicts a house with a simple triangular pitched roof, the kind drawn by almost any child. The early Greeks abstracted this symbol so that it became a double roof on its side, which in turn became the familiar double dome on our 'B'. *Delta*, meanwhile, a triangle, represented a door ('daleth' in the early Semitic languages, and 'Delet' is a door in modern Hebrew). The triangle presumably depicts an opening in a tent. Meanwhile, the Semitic 'He', which became *epsilon*, our 'E', represented a latticed window. Add a vertical line to the right of the letter and you can see the familiar shape of a sash window – a simplification but a useful one. Then there is 'Waw' or 'Vav', which evolved into our 'F', the pictograph being a tent-peg or hook, the form of which can still be seen in our letter, just as we can still see the form of a section of fence in our 'H', which derives from the Semitic 'Heth', meaning a fence or barrier – it is also incidentally related to the Phoenician 'Hasir', our courtyard.

The centrality of the house to the development of language indicates the depth to which the form of the dwelling is embedded in our culture and in our most basic tools of communication.

Nevertheless, Jung's idea of a collective unconscious remains controversial. Do we all really have within us a reservoir of symbols and archetypes that have survived and thrived through our species for millennia? Is the house an expression of a series of elements which allows us to root ourselves not only to a fixed place in a world of flux and insecurity but in a continuum of historical allusion and metaphor, a system of signs and symbols built up to become part of a folk consciousness we don't even realize we have? The very idea of a collective consciousness is fraught with the potential for dangerous deviation. Many of the authors whose work represents the most articulate espousal of these ideas drifted conspicuously to the right. Heidegger was famously a member of the Nazi party from an early date. The Romanian scholar Mircea Eliade, whose explorations of ritual and meaning in building and the perception of space – notably *The Sacred and the Profane* (1957) – are among the finest there are, was similarly tainted by his outspoken support of the savage Iron Guard. The idea of a cultural lineage expressed through an existential architecture can easily elide into a kind of nationalist dogma, the kind of medieval mythologizing the Nazis were over-fond of. But those associations shouldn't be allowed to spoil the notion that the things that surround us can be containers of meaning. We must attempt to circumvent the national and the local and to consider not just mythology, superstition and folklore but the wider cultural world of film and literature, TV, videos, comics and pop-dream interpretation, alongside psychology, sociology and fairy tales. These images and ideas saturate our culture and create for us a world of meaning if we are only dimly aware of it.

In this book I'd like to propose that, no matter how mundane, how clichéd or over-familiar the most basic elements of our homes might be, they contain within them a rich history of meaning and allusion that enables us to feel fixed in time and place but also in folk and popular mythology, in memories which might be our own or which might come from films or photoshoots, to place ourselves in a world of the familiar and occasionally the extraordinary. Our lives and our relationship to our objects and our interiors have changed radically over recent years, more radically perhaps than at any period for millennia. We are used to living in the three dimensions of the physical space of our homes – though we have often become blasé to the fourth dimension of time, which is at least as important. But we have now introduced into our homes a fifth dimension of cyberspace, which allows us to be connected to everything everywhere simultaneously. Our homes, however, have changed surprisingly little. Perhaps we need the spaces that surround us to embody a continuity in contrast to the changes in technology which increasingly dominate our time at work and at leisure.

My contention here is that our houses and homes, no matter what style they are realized in, no matter how modest or seemingly ill-considered their architecture, are vessels of an extraordinary history, perhaps the last repositories of a language of symbol and collective memory that ties us to our ancestors, to profound and ancient threads of meaning. We may not know where these symbols come from, what they mean or how they came to look the way they do, but their presence enriches the landscape of our lives and, as I hope to show, they remain fundamental to our idea of a home.

Dwelling is both place and process. The idea, that our lives can be 'read' through our homes, through their decoration, their design and their contents, infiltrates popular culture.

At one time, objects defined us far more clearly. Every 'thing' had a purpose and its centrality to the rituals of everyday life made it a vessel for containing meaning. Architect Aldo van Eyck once described the phenomenon of 'basket-house-village-universe', in which everything, even the smallest, most quotidian receptacle, expresses ideas about our being in the world, our picture of the cosmos. Now we have so much more 'stuff' and so many technological devices for which no deeper cultural language of meaning has yet developed, that the individual items might seem to have lost their symbolic potency. This makes the image of the house even more important.

There is certainly nothing new about the idea of 'reading' architecture. There are plenty of books that purport to allow the reader to interpret the story of a gothic church ('a Bible in stone' goes the cliché) or a grand country house. In fact there has recently been an explosion of literature in which buildings become symbolic labyrinths to be decoded by poorly drawn and unlikely academic heroes. Dan Brown's barely readable *The Da Vinci Code* and its semi-parodic, often numbingly banal imitators, have, despite their faults, reawakened in us to the idea that architecture can be a repository of occult meanings, a blend of masonic mumbo-jumbo, conspiracy theory and half-remembered art history. It is an artistic (or more accurately pulp) archetype that re-emerges every few years, from *The Omen* to *Tomb Raider*, an idea that buildings can embody arcane knowledge and give up their secrets to reveal treasure, horror or revelation. It was there in Marlowe's *Dr Faustus* and it is there in the psychogeography of Peter Ackroyd or Iain Sinclair. But it is usually applied to buildings of religious or historic significance or landscapes of the sublime or the desolate. There are readings of the numerical significance of the proportions of a Greek temple or a gothic cathedral, the symbolic schema of a Roman basilica or a Renaissance cupola, an idea of a knowledge once familiar to masons and masterbuilders, which we have forgotten and for the forgetting of which we are the poorer. There are readings of heraldic devices and there are 'house detectives' to help is reveal the history of old homes.

Here, I am not concerned with buildings of great status, the special and the particular. I hope that we can begin to show that, while it is obviously far easier to read the iconography of a church or a temple than an apartment or a mobile home, the trickle-down drip of symbolism has a long history and much more of it survives in even the smallest apartment than you might imagine.

At the risk of sounding like a crank, there is something compelling in the notion of an arcane, lost knowledge but it is present rather in an attitude to building and dwelling than in architecture as a container of occult knowledge. Roman and medieval builders had a very different attitude to the construction of a house. A building was seen as a living, organic thing. If you're ever passing a building site and there are some workers celebrating on the roof around a spindly tree, that will be a 'topping out' ceremony. This old ritual marks the moment a building becomes watertight. The tree is a symbol of the beginning of its new life and it is a sacrifice. I recently drank tepid cava from a plastic beaker at the topping out of an office tower, a building you would think soulless, yet its construction was still deemed by those who put the effort into building it as deserving of a ritual. The banal architecture of the everyday, the buildings in the background are as physically demanding to build as the serious stuff and just as deserving of ritual.

Historically, buildings were not only considered magical in themselves, they also sheltered spirits who needed to be appeased. The reason we say 'bless you' when someone sneezes is that the devil was thought to exploit that vulnerable moment after a sneeze to inveigle himself into your soul. In the same way, a house would be blessed – to keep the devil out and to assuage the spirits of the earth and the place. We may still hold a housewarming or put a wreath on our doors at Christmas but, in earlier times, living sacrifices were made to appease evil spirits. Once mummified cats might be buried beneath the floor or chickens slaughtered so that their blood spilled onto the threshold. Those animal sacrifices transmuted over time to a coin buried under the building; you can still find old pennies beneath Victorian doorways, which is a good luck sacrifice. The 'time capsules' (a.k.a. coffee cans stuffed with junk) buried in gardens by generations of children can be seen as a successor to the sacrifice to place, to an idea of continuity. Builders, until quite recently, used to regularly bury sheets of that day's newspaper beneath flooring, which – when it is not purely functional, is a similar gesture of marking time.

As well the tenacious and surprising survival of these arcane rituals, there is the more obvious role of the home as the projection of self. The façade is, quite literally, the face, the expression with windows for eyes and a door for a mouth and, once inside, each room has its role in the representation of a part of our inner lives. The hall represents a shadow of the time when a home was a single living space containing every activity; it announces arrival and departure. The kitchen is a space of transformation and alchemy, of raw materials into sustenance, but it is also the space of the mother and of refuge, the warm, secure womb. The bedroom is fraught with a complex symbolism of birth, sleep, sex, dreams and death. The cellar represents the dark recesses of the subconscious upon which our public lives are precariously built; its counterpart is the attic, with memories and secrets of the past. And so on.

The idea of meaning in architecture has, over the last century or so, become rather unfashionable. Modernist architecture constituted an attempt to remake buildings, to abandon the dark recesses and patterned wallpapers of the Victorian bourgeois interior in favour of a clean, clear architecture of light and fluid space. Walter Benjamin described the architecture of the *fin de siècle* as the construction of places of *traces*. If Heidegger equated dwelling with building, Benjamin described living as the leaving of traces of ourselves. He suggested that the rise of the detective novel as the art form of modernity indicated that the clues, the personal artefacts and the marks and barely visible remnants of our presence and actions in the home would be all that was left. That traces are the best we could leave suggests a melancholic despair at the lack of impact our lives would have, yet it is precisely in the home that we are able to leave those marks. Benjamin interpreted the Modernist urge towards an architecture of glass and transparency as a move to obliterate even those few traces of our selves from the domestic realm. He looked to vitrines and cabinets, to plush-lined cases for glasses or cutlery where our things had left impressions, to dust and the faded wallpaper behind a painting as indications of life as lived.

A house is a museum, an exhibition of the changes in the way life has been lived. Historians strip back layers of wallpaper in old houses to discover the successions of colour schemes, from arsenic green (the wallpaper colouring which could kill, as it allegedly did for Napoleon) to curry-house maroon flock. A house is like a body which can be dressed in layers, which can be stripped and changed, made up and tattooed. But it can also be changed right to its core. Extensions and attics, cellars dug below, conservatories added on, houses are constantly being adapted to meet the needs of changing lifestyles. Kitchens, once functional and mean, are now representational spaces: expansive, light and airy, filled with expensive equipment over-specified for an age of takeaways, pizza deliveries and microwaves. Bathrooms have sprung up all over the house, in bedrooms, downstairs, in attics; and another functional, cold space has become a room for pampering and luxury. Each subsequent change maps the presence, the taste and the life of the occupier, becomes a manifestation of identity, a passport stamp. DIY and the will to shape the house becomes a substitute for a life which we might often feel is beyond our control. Oppressed by work, the state, by family and financial obligations the contemporary homeowner can feel that the house is the one field of expression and freedom open to them. Particularly for the increasingly emasculated male, the house can become the one visible trace of his existence, the thing he has to show for a life of hard work, whether that work is done by his own hands or by the hands of others.

This then makes it all the more surprising that so many homes end up looking exactly the same. Flip through a London estate agent's brochure and you'll see endless variations of Victorian terraces extended and renovated using the same palette of materials and spaces, a bland modernity imposed on the rear of every stock brick back extension, a curious collision of tradition and Modernism which seems to be the balance the Brits like – historic front, glass back, displaying tradition to the world and commercial modernity to the garden.

In the US, homeowners tend to be more mobile and their houses newer. Many have never lived in a house that wasn't new or almost new, yet the houses they will have lived in are as traditional in form as those Victorian terraces, simulacra of a blend of prairie, colonial, Victorian and Levittown, and they contain as many layers of meaning and symbol as their older European counterparts because each house draws on the same traditional archetypes. Of course, just as the revolving fashionable tropes of contemporary renovation and extension display wealth and the ability to keep up with, or ahead of, the neighbours, so decline indicates a deeper existential despair. The peeling paint and mouldy curtains, spalling plaster and unkempt state of a property suggests the inhabitant has lost the will the engage with the world, it is synonymous with decline. In Edgar Allen Poe's *The Fall of the House of Usher*, the 'house' is both the family and the physical dwelling. With windows like eyes and a huge, dark fissure opening up its front wall, the gothic house represents the disturbed mental state of the narrator's old friend Roderick Usher. In the same way Miss Havisham's dusty, decrepit house in Dickens' *Great Expectations* is a metaphor for madness, as is the tumbledown house in which Boo Radley lived in *To Kill a Mockingbird*. Even more epic is the decline mapped out in the establishing shots *Citizen Kane* showing Charles Foster Kane's house, Xanadu, a symbol of hubris and the fleeting nature of even the most astonishing wealth and influence. When Kane dies the house remains unfinished yet already in decline, a metaphor for unfulfilled ambition and disappointment – Kane's final words relate not to his huge house but to his childhood sled, christened 'Rosebud', which was incinerated in the furnace in the vast cellars beneath the house, in the depths of the subconscious which Freud would compare to repressed memory.

There has recently been a rash of novels in which the house, the home, the block or the street becomes a cipher for its inhabitants, for the state of the city and society and of the changing nature of community and the complex network of relationships within it. John Lanchester's *Capital* (2012) uses a London street and its increasingly expensive houses (and their embodied value) as the symbol of a changing city. Aravind Adiga's *Last Man in Tower* (2011) meanwhile sees the decaying Mumbai apartment block as a cipher for a civilized middle class community within the chaos of the city and demonstrates how quickly that veneer of civilization breaks down through the desire for the money a developers offers to its residents to leave so he can redevelop the site. Will Wiles' *Care of Wooden Floors* (2012) the litany of interiors disasters which occur in an apartment the protagonist is looking after for a friend begin to represent a looming personal crisis. The intimate link between home and being provides novelists and film makers with a way of sketching character in more dimensions than just the personal. The world of space and objects, the realm of the home becomes the perfect parallel plane of projection.

Homes are also, of course, made of memories. Their reality lies not so much in their physicality but in the images we have of precious or painful moments within their walls. Our childhood homes colour our perception of every subsequent space we inhabit and they condition our responses, either encouraging us to recreate the rooms of our pasts or to react against them. But it turns out that our memories are more closely tied in with our minds than mere nostalgia. Recent fascinating research from the University of Notre Dame in Indiana has indicated that a very familiar problem with which every one of us is surely familiar, that of walking into a room and forgetting what it was you had gone in there for, might be connected with the act of actually passing through the door itself. The door, it appears, triggers a change. What has become known as the 'doorway effect' seems to be the mind's way of compartmentalizing certain information, you have moved away from one room so the information connected with that room has now become less important, it has shifted into the past and what is connected with the new room is now what is important. In this way the brain manages to prioritize bits of information, making certain things easier to retrieve. It is the only way it can cope with the vast amount of data fed into it. Intriguingly the same effect is felt if those taking part in the experiment move through a virtual door in a computer game or simulation.

This effect is very much related to the idea of the 'memory palace'. This is a mnemonic device initially documented by Roman rhetoricians (notably Cicero and Quintilian) in which facts and ideas are mentally placed in rooms in an imaginary or a remembered, real house, home or palace. Tony Judt, the historian who suffered from Lou Gehrig's disease and became paralysed from the neck down, entitled his dying memoir *The Memory Chalet*, organizing his memories around the nooks and corners, rooms and spaces of the Swiss chalet he stayed in as a child while on skiing holidays with his parents. It seems our minds are conditioned to respond particularly to the arrangement of a dwelling, that the bond between our brains and our homes is as real as the physical need for shelter and comfort.

We are extraordinarily sensitive to the sights, smells, textures and sensations of our homes. We pick up the slightest changes, we recognize the odours of individual homes – each of which is delicately, subtly different, a blend of cooking, cleaning, damp, age and myriad other factors. Each room within a house will have its own smell, its own temperature, its own feel. The comedian Steven Wright used to tell a gag about everything in his apartment having been stolen and replaced with an exact replica. This touches on a sense of the uncanny, a heightened sensitivity of awareness about our own homes in which things feel right – or wrong. We can detect the slightest changes, feel when something is not right. Our bond with our homes can be quite extraordinary.

In this book I have written almost exclusively about Western traditions because those are the customs, architectures and histories I am familiar with. But it would in many ways be easier to write this kind of book about Eastern homes. The traditions of Feng Shui in China and Vastu Shastra in India are familiar, if perhaps only superficially understood, and they codify a huge array of customs and traditions for how a home, a temple, a village or a city should be built and arranged. Much of it is common sense with regard to site, topography, the weather and so on. But much more of it also embodies a compendium of social and cultural taboos, a mapping through building of the development of a culture. In the writings of Vitruvius, the Roman architect living in the first century BC, we also see this careful codification of building and meaning and we know from the drawings, diagrams and notes of medieval masons that they too had an extraordinary knowledge of proportion, structure, decoration and an understanding of architecture as a system of signs and a means of communication. The humblest of builders right up to the industrialization of the eighteenth and nineteenth centuries and the mass migrations to the new centres of work similarly retained an understanding of what the parts of a home *meant*. But we have almost entirely lost that knowledge. Or at least it can *seem* as if we have lost that knowledge. My contention is that in fact these meanings, symbols and signs are buried so deep within us, in our collective subconscious, that in fact we are quite able to understand, relate and respond to the elements of domestic symbolism even though we may not know it. These meanings are now just transmitted in different ways. They come to us via movies and books, photography and art, through memory and association, via the pages of magazines and through our familiarity with the homes of our friends and acquaintances, with our trips to historic houses and to museums and with an innate understanding of what a home means.

We have also, though, undergone a transformation in the way we regard out homes. Our homes were once the centres of almost every important event in our lives, its rooms marked the rites of passage involved in being born and giving birth, in growing up and in work, in getting married, getting old and dying. Most of these have now been taken out of the home. The medicalization of birth, death and illness, and the honeymoon holiday, have taken all of the major rites of passage out of the home. We might still work at home but it is rare compared to the days when the vast majority of people plied their crafts in the home, lived above the shop, lived with their livestock and on their farms. Our homes have become dormitories, places to sleep and perhaps relax but they are still the venues for certain rituals, for Christmas or the celebration of religious holidays, for occasions on which families get together and so on. But perhaps the most alienating aspect of contemporary existence and the one that has most radically changed the nature of our relationship to home is the perception of a dwelling as an asset. Houses are viewed as potential development projects, changes are made not to accommodate the rituals of daily life but to add value – financial and not existential value. As our homes, whether they are rented or owned, account for such a huge proportion of our income, this is understandable but it does not help us to see the home in terms of meaning but rather in value and in fashion. But the value of houses can go down as well as up.

I suggest that we ignore the symbolism and significance of the elements of domestic architecture to our own detriment. Homes might collapse in financial value just as they might rise and it is unwise for us to see them as utilitarian investment vehicles to the exclusion of everything else. Instead we should see them as receptacles of both personal and collective memory, containers of meaning and symbol, as theatrical sets against which the dramas of our lives are enacted. That way, even as the value of your home may plummet, at least you can console yourself with the knowledge that it remains unimaginably rich in meaning.

The essays are based on a series which has been appearing in the *Financial Times* (for which I am the Architecture Critic) since 2008 so there might be a little repetition and some of you might have read some of this material before but I hope there is enough that is new here to make it worth the reader's while.

ACKNOWLEDGMENTS

I'd like to thank my wife, Krisztina, for her patience and tolerance of life with a writer. I'd also like to thank my father, Graham Heathcote, for inculcating in me a love of books and words and inadvertently helping me to begin to see books as a building material. And my mother for putting up with my father.

I would never have become interested in the subject of meaning in architecture without my tutor at Kingston University Trevor Garnham, whom I would like to thank for introducing me to W.R. Lethaby.

I also need to thank my editors at the *Financial Times*, Alison Beard and subsequently Jane Owen, for their support in continuing to allow me to publish these rather indulgent pieces – which I think no other paper would have published and to the *Financial Times* itself for allowing me to use these pieces as the basis of this book. Finally I'd like to thank my children, Lili and Ella for their patience whilst I finish off writing yet another piece.

1   FRONT DOORS

Even the most ordinary element of the most mundane of houses can carry within it memories and layers of culture and history, meanings and symbols. That we have lost the ability to read them makes our lives poorer and has stolen from us the capacity to engage with our surroundings on a level more meaningful than that of the image. Take a door – a good, solid, panelled Georgian door. One of the most familiar will do just fine: the shiny black door of 10 Downing Street.

The door is a crossing, a junction marking the divide between the realm of the public and the private, between the chaos of the unformed world outside and the sacrosanct order within, and as such it represents a profoundly symbolic moment that needs to be marked.

The doors of temples or grand houses used to be oriented towards the rising sun to catch the morning rays (the word 'orientation', towards the east, derives from this). It was a kind of sacred awakening; opening the door, a mini-ritual, welcomed in the sun and the light of the new day. The primal fear of pre-enlightenment societies was that the sun wouldn't rise anew the next morning. The Egyptians envisaged the passage of the sun through the underworld as a journey between two gates beneath us. The door became the earthly equivalent of those sun gates.

Each time the sun rose again it was a cause for small celebration and thanksgiving.

Later this significance became translated into symbolic, material form. The temple doors of Rome were clad in gilt bronze, and the arches above Byzantine doorways of Venice are adorned with golden mosaics or carvings of the sun and moon. This tribute transmogrified into a more modest brass threshold that would be polished each morning to reflect the light. These can still be seen in Victorian terraces as much as in gentlemen's clubs. Brass is the quotidian version of gold, the material manifestation of the sun. Now take a look at that Downing Street door. It is adorned with a lion's head doorknocker (in brass, of course). The lion was similarly the symbol of the sun, his golden mane a plume of flame. Above the door a fan light with radiating glazing bars once again symbolically represents the rising sun, behind the glass you can just make out the wrought-iron rays of a protective grille tapering into nothing.

As if all this weren't enough, a lantern hangs suspended above the door so that even at night the meaning remains clear and is reinforced by the light emanating from the false sun of the fanlight, a symbol of protection from darkness.

The door leaf itself is the element within architecture that represents the resident. It imposes human scale on the façade and, as such, is vaguely anthropomorphic in form. Its tripartite division (legs, body, head) are there in the panels, while at its centre the doorknob as navel and the letterbox as, well, perhaps that'll do for the moment.

It might seem a plain kind of door, but in the Spartan, stripped-back tradition of Georgian building, the door was effectively the only element that could be embellished. The sparse bare brick walls, self-effacing windows and parapet concealing the form of the roof left only the entrance as a decorative element.

Its knobs and knockers, fanlight and panels were the language of humanization, and although it may seem a modest kind of ornamentation, because the architecture is so plain, any decorative elements at all take on far greater symbolic and social significance than they otherwise might on a more decorated structure.

The fanlight survives today in the cheapest of catalogue doors, now transposed on to the door leaf itself, a motif which makes no architectural sense at all (the semi-circular opening reflects the structural brick arch above) but which retains within it the memory of that sun-like archetype. The panels are still present too, now pressed into a mulch of fibres stiffened into pseudo-timber with glue and powder, again retaining only the vaguest memory of the door's original construction. Doors were made of a solid timber frame infilled with slightly thinner panels. This made the door lighter and cheaper to construct from more slender timbers but also created an elegant decorative plane with a deceptively complex language of mouldings and chamfers.

The lion's head knocker has survived as a DIY staple whilst the lantern above has moved to the side to become the almost poetically clichéd coachlight. The front door embodies ownership, expressing the occupant. The handing over of keys remains a hugely symbolic moment, whilst their insertion carries unmissable sexual undertones and the sacrality of crossing is maintained in the custom of carrying the bride over the threshold. The strange meaning behind this ritual is the avoidance of evil spirits which were thought to lurk in the liminal zone of the threshold, a boundary which is neither within nor without. For a bride to trip on her first entry to the house would have been seen as a dreadful omen, a portent of bad luck to come, and a possibility best avoided. It is extraordinary how widespread this custom is; it is one of the few traditions to cross cultural boundaries around the world.

The ghost of Jacob Marley famously appears to Scrooge in the brass knocker, a manifestation of the spirit of the threshold. The threshold itself is a curious survivor. Its purpose is both symbolic and functional. It would have once served to stop water entering the dwelling and also perhaps to fix the doorframe in place. But it is the most critical boundary of the dwelling, a thin line demarcating the public and the private. To cross it uninvited is to trespass, to commit a crime. The diminution of the architectural expression of the threshold (who now polishes brass or marble doorsteps?) has led to its symbolic significance being replaced by the doormat. This prickly carpet is similarly a symbolic moment, the point of a ritual cleansing of the shoes before entering the sacred realm of the home. To wipe your feet is a mark of respect. The cast-iron boot scrapers built into the porches of some houses presents another ritual (although once very practical) moment. It is comparable to the stoup in a church – a water receptacle often similarly built into a recess in the wall in the narthex of a church. The dipping of the finger into the holy water and the making of the sign of the cross is a moment of ritual, if not real, cleansing, just as are the mat and the scraper. At the entrance to 10 Downing Street there are a pair of cast iron bootscrapers, one to either side of the door – they have a sun motif at their tops. Then there is the rarer survival of the red carpet laid out for auspicious guests, another symbolic setting out of a privileged route but also an extension of the interior to the exterior – a sign that for this visitor the house is open and welcoming – which is exactly what the 'Welcome' door mat does.

Many of the doors contemporary with Number 10 would have had steps leading up to the door, a device to bridge the area which gave light to the basement windows below but which also allowed the elevation of the ground floor above the filth and ordure which covered the streets. These steps also create a space apart, an idea that this is the way in to somewhere special. In Dutch houses of the seventeenth and eighteenth century – which share their sparse, protestant aesthetic with those of London, the device was made more of in the creation of a stoop. This has nothing to do with the stoup in a church but is rather an elevated plane which bridges the realm of the city and the realm of the interior. It was the Dutch who effectively invented the bourgeois interior (so beautifully depicted in the art of the era) and the subtlety of this distinction, the creation of an in-between zone of semi-public and semi-private interaction between the two worlds, is characteristic of the sophistication of Dutch architecture. This was a place often provided with a built-in bench (many of these can still be seen on the streets of Amsterdam) where a traveller or tradesman could wait or rest or where a housewife could talk to her neighbours or a gentleman could smoke his pipe while watching the world outside. The stoop (its etymology derives simply from the German for 'step') was adopted by the Dutch settlers in America and then by their British successors and it became an archetype of a mythical big city lifestyle. People sitting on their stoops create and reinforce community and maintain their own policing of the streets.

The front door – and the area around it – remains a strange and powerfully enduring reminder of superstition and myth. The survival of the most recognisable of domestic motifs into an era when both their constructional and symbolic logic has long disappeared is extraordinary. The cheapest, mass-produced, pressed and formed MDF door leaves still embody worlds of long-lost symbolism. Sun worship, demons and omens, fear, light, sex, life and death are all expressed in an architectural element that has become so familiar that its articulation has become invisible to us. And that's just the door.

2

HALLS

THE HALL WAS ONCE all there was. The hall-house of medieval England was a roof, open to the rafters, over a single barn of a space. It was the space for eating and sleeping, for receiving guests, for cooking, for relaxing and for celebrating. So how did the hall become reduced to the meagre, dingy, windowless corridor familiar from emasculated modern apartments and housing? A leftover lobby reserved more for the human husks of coats and shoes rather than for the human beings themselves?

The medieval hall, despite being a single space, had its own internal hierarchy. A microcosmic version of the nave of a church, a big hall featured a raised dais (the equivalent of a sanctuary) rather like a stage, upon which the master and his family would dine and possibly sleep. Oxford and Cambridge colleges, with their High Table, retain the clear memory of this arrangement, as does the idea of a 'top table' at a wedding or reception. The hall gradually atrophied in importance as the Great Chamber, a (slightly) more private bedroom, emerged. But it remained the symbol of the householder's status, the principal public room. As dwellings morphed first into mansions and then into urban houses the staircase appeared, growing from the floor of the hall like a tree supporting the upper floors.

The arrival of the staircase – in the finest houses a grand, sculptural statement – radically altered the nature of the hall. It became a circulation space, the room of introduction, movement and transition. Intriguingly, the etymology of 'hall' ('*heall*' or 'covered place' in Old English) is the same as 'hell'. The hall, to paraphrase Sartre, is other people.

It is in essence a social space, the internal, domestic equivalent of the town square. The coats, boots and umbrellas, and the stone or marble floors, were a reminder of its nature as an interface between the interior and the exterior. Only a generation ago, a hall table would have always been crowned with a telephone, more evidence of its border condition between the worlds of the public and the private.

In the terraced house or apartment, the hall retains the memory of its former grandeur, there may be a dappling of light from a stained glass porch window, the only place stained glass is likely to appear, or perhaps from a fanlight above the door. A mirror often adorns the wall, the last vestige of the decoration that would have once announced and reflected the act of entrance, whilst the newel on the balustrade, crowned by a wooden globe, stands like a memory of a footman. The hall generated its own particular species of curious furniture – the half-tables and consoles squashed against the wall, the hall stands, benches and trunks that are often placed more in order to populate this under-used space than to be themselves used. Each contributes to the idea of the hall as a place purely intended to project character, its own use never explicitly defined. But they also constitute an odd taxonomy of surreal items that mean nothing on their own but can exist only when used in conjunction with the walls squeezing a narrow space. The hall stand, that combination of umbrella holder, coat and hat stand and mirror is a typically hybrid, attenuated object like the half console table, which looks as if it might also poke into the hall next door.

Apartments contain a more complex layering of symbol and use as the boundaries between public space, residents-only space and the realm of the explicitly private build up. The well-to-do New York apartment block offers an intriguing series of transitions from street to home: the carpet, the canopy, the doorman, a plush lobby visible through glass but not accessible from the street (but which acts as a formal reception space for waiting), the elevator, the lobby, and only then the hall. It is a complex choreography of transition, echoed in slightly less hierarchical terms in the London mansion block or the Parisian apartment building, and it is a typology that owes much to the idea of the grand hotel as the ideal dwelling, projecting a fantasy of service and luxury onto a public face. The communal hall, like its relative the lobby, is a functionally useless place, built purely to impress adorned with marble surfaces, sconces, flowers, it bears that anonymous, under-used luxury of a hotel. Yet it also creates that critical first impression, a moment of architectural theatre, setting the scene.

Hermann Muthesius, a German writer whose 1905 book *The English House* held up British domestic architecture as the finest in the world, noted that the hall represented 'one of the most attractive assets of the English House. . . . The particular form of the hall', he wrote, was the 'elaboration of a romantic chain of thought' weaving 'a special magic round this room'.

If Muthesius represented the warmth and memory of the hall as a place of humanity and domestic embrace, the Danish artist Vilhelm Hammershoi painted its opposite in the same year: the cool, existential crisis of emptiness exemplified in

White Doors. Here, the hall appears as a place of cold neutrality, empty of people and furniture, eerie, haunting, presaging an age of angst and social isolation.

Ultimately, the hall, however grand, is leftover space. It is the area that needs to be devoted to necessary circulation rather than actual life. In that way it embodies a curious position between grudging acceptance (which always leads to it being too small and mean) and ostentatious grandeur (which is a naked display of wealth – a gesture to show that the owners are so wealthy they can afford to waste space). In either case the hall occupies an odd, liminal position and one that is always curiously underutilized. Why shouldn't it become a space for living? As the most public part of the dwelling its role as mere transitional space seems a waste. Celebrate it.

3

LIVING ROOMS

L IVING ROOM, AS OPPOSED, I used to wonder, to what exactly? Not living room? Living dead room? Dying room? Dead room?

Well, yes, it turns out. Exactly. The living room is the modern, sanitized term for the parlour, the formal room at the front of the house (front room). This is the room that was once reserved for special occasions, and one special occasion more than any other – death. The bodies of deceased family members were laid out on biers or trestles for a wake, a final domestic resting place before burial. A room that was to provide a place for the dead demanded a certain decorum, a dignity, this was a room not merely to be enjoyed, or even much inhabited, but one in which to be respectable. The family's treasures, its art, its best furniture and carpets, the objects through which their achievements could be read were strewn about this room, protected from the outside by heavy shutters and drapes.

Today it seems a curious conceit that the best room in the house be given over, in effect, to the dead, yet traces of this idea of decorum, of the maintenance of a 'best' room in the manner of a 'best' suit remain. In working class households until recently life was often lived in the kitchen – the only consistently heated space in the house – where people ate, read, bathed and met

34

their neighbours – who came in from the back alley. The front room was preserved – like the cellophane-shrouded three-piece suite – for best. A film like *Saturday Night and Sunday Morning* illustrates this perfectly, this was the realm of the fearsome matriarch vigilantly controlling the social and spatial flows.

The middle classes and those aspiring to middle class existence used their living rooms more, though they too almost certainly maintained a room for best. If we look at Robert S. Tait's painting *Thomas and Jane Carlyle in the Living Room of their House in Cheyne Row, Chelsea* (1857) we see a couple looking rather bored, despite being, of course, two of the most interesting Victorians. Carlyle is playing with his pipe by the fireplace; Jane is sitting, staring in a chair. It has the muted feel of a dull Sunday even though the room itself is spacious and bright, its double doors open to reveal the rest of the house. Ironically, the living room is the also deadest room. It is a feel that remains almost unchanged for another century. Think of Celia Johnson's character in *Brief Encounter* on the verge of a breakdown with her decent, dull husband doing a crossword in his armchair – classic suburban torpor – or of Pooter in his dull Holloway suburban living room ('The Laurels') or of the unbearably oppressive boredom of the living room in Bryan Forbes' 1964 *Séance on a Wet Afternoon*. You can flit between early Victorian and Kitchen Sink drama to get the impression of an ill-used, awkward kind of place, which can seem strange to us.

In the Georgian era the front room was situated on the *piano nobile*, elevated to the first floor, looking down on the world, and this was a room for entertaining, for dining, for dancing. The Victorians, however, moved it back down and the front room became a very Victorian kind of façade, a room intended to project an image to the world, far more about presentation than about use. It became the most highly decorated room, with masses of ornate furniture, pictures, mouldings, perhaps a frieze and a tiled and cast-iron fireplace. But it also became dusty, musty and dim. In recent years this internal apartheid between a front and rear parlour (and often kitchen too) has been eroded as occupants have knocked through the ground floor to create a single living space, albeit one which is often curiously misaligned and unsettlingly asymmetrical.

The modern era has seen the focus of the room shift from the coffin to the box.

There were formerly three foci for the living room: the window (which gave light by which to read), the fireplace (the domestic altar which gave warmth but which also acted as a kind of shrine, the mantelpiece of museum of memories and mementoes) and the piano. These have been replaced entirely by the TV, which has somehow never quite been incorporated into the architecture – as if acknowledging its centrality to everyday life is some kind of admission of failure. This has unbalanced the contemporary living room entirely. We have sofas looking into what appears to be a void. This is why, ironically, these rooms work so well on TV: the ensemble looking at the TV – us looking back at them. Whether it belongs to the Simpsons or to the Royle family, the TV-focused sofa has become shorthand for the blue-collar dwelling, amiable slobbishness.

Eating in front of the TV, we are often told, has killed conversation (over 50 per cent of families in the UK and the US eat more meals in front of the TV than together than at the table), which is ironic, as one of the living room's other names is the 'parlour' from the French *parler*, to talk. Yet, in a curious way, contemporary trends have revived the Victorian tradition of the front room as a representative space. Minimal interiors in which every gadget is hidden once more become 'clean' rooms, rooms for 'best'. Architects and magazines have popularized a minimal aesthetic, which seems to preclude the stuff of everyday life, so these spaces remain pristine. The real living in contemporary homes is increasingly done in the kitchens (as it once was in the working-class terrace). The proliferation of TVs and of computer and console-stuffed bedrooms and dens has ensured that the slippery symbolism of cyberspace is increasingly affecting real space. Elsewhere the dominant aesthetic of the loft has eroded traditional distinctions between spaces, so that the hierarchies of types of living room that were so intriguing to read – of drawing rooms and billiard rooms, smoking rooms, libraries and parlours – are disappearing. As the walls disappear, the house gets harder to read, the story less interesting and less revealing. But that ubiquitous contemporary urge towards a flow of space does begin to show the extraordinary and enduring influence of Modernism and how we attempt to apply it even to the most historic of our buildings. It may look like the hierarchy of houses is getting harder to read but in fact we are just superimposing another layer of meaning, the importance of the appearance of the Modern.

4

FIREPLACES

IT IS NO COINCIDENCE that the Greek goddess Hestia and her Roman equivalent Vesta were associated not just with the hearth but with the home. This domestic goddess was also responsible for the knowledge of building houses, of domestic construction, and in the Roman and Greek home the hearth was far more than a functional fitting; it was a kind of eternal flame, guarded by, and dedicated to, the gods. The flames were never allowed to subside, unless ritually to be renewed again and Vesta (and those famous Vestal Virgins) were the guardians.

Prometheus suffered terrible agonies (his liver being pecked out by a vulture for all eternity) to bring Mankind fire, so the flames had to be treated with respect. And still should. The hearth and the fireplace are as close as the contemporary secular Western dwelling comes to a shrine. The flames are contained in a kind of aedicule, a miniature house within which they lick and burn, a structure that is a simulacrum of the dwelling itself. In fact you could argue that the house arose as a shelter for the fire as much as it did for humans – it was the fire that was crucial to life rather than the roof. The notion that the fireplace forms the 'focus' of the domestic interior has passed into estate agent and interior design cliché, yet it is far more profound in its own way than we might realize. The Greek word for hearth is in fact *focus*.

And that is firmly what it remains. Incidentally, the French word *foyer* shares the same root.

The first household fires would have been freestanding, situated in a pit or a pot at the heart of the dwelling, the smoke they generated rising up through an oculus in the roof (*oculus* is literally an 'eye' to the sky). The mysterious element of fire was thus allowed to commune between the heavens and the earth, a memory of Prometheus's act of generosity. The Greek *focus* would have burnt in a shallow bowl, appearing as a kind of ritual offering offered up in a dish, like the blood of a slaughtered animal. The 'eternal flames' that still burn in memorials around the world continue to use this same architectural and decorative language.

You could, I suppose, argue that the flickering blue flame of the gas pilot light conveys the same purpose as the eternal flame, yet this is never celebrated, always banished to a cupboard beneath the stairs or well out of the way, a thing to be hidden and denied.

The fire at the centre of the home would, in ancient times, also have been eternal. The difficulty of re-kindling a fire would have meant that a flame would have been kept burning, and the extinction of the flames would have been perceived as a bad omen. In Greece the flames were symbolically carried by the bride's mother from her home fire to the dwelling of the newlyweds to ensure a continuity of domesticity – the hearth being seen as the centre of married life. The hearth remained the realm of the mistress of the house, but this is not to be confused with the kitchen fire. The hearth was the dwelling place of the gods and the spirit of the house, to cook on it would have been to pollute its purity; cooking was done elsewhere. The one time the flames were ritually allowed to subside was on the death of the house's owner.

Towards the end of the twelfth century, though, the invention of the chimney radically changed the nature of the dwelling and the place of the fire within it. The chimney is, arguably, the most important architectural invention since the roof. The chimneypiece became the literal focus of the great halls of the medieval era, works of architecture in their own right. Set into the deep stone walls, an arch above, it became a kind of counterpoint to the windows, a view to a different, more ethereal world of light and heat. The decoration of the surround emphasized the centrality and importance of the fire to life. This was the invention that separated men from beasts, which made us human, and the verticality of the chimney poking up above the roof is a reflection of man's upright position in the world.

The hoods above the hearth in particular became more and more ornamented, bearing coats of arms and elaborate carvings. In a big hall the heat was quickly dissipated so, in acknowledgement of the centrality of the fire as the most desirable place in the dwelling, the inglenook emerged, effectively a room within a room. It reached its zenith in the British Arts and Crafts era when the inglenook became the image of a nostalgic, intimate domesticity, a place to retreat on a cold day with a book and toasted crumpets. In the sublime work of M.H. Baillie Scott, Edwin Lutyens, W.R. Lethaby, and Charles Rennie Mackintosh (also of Adolf Loos in Austria and of the American Arts and Crafts architects) the inglenook became the defining motif of an architecture which was paradoxically at once historicizing and nostalgic and revelling in its English folksiness, while also being a spur for the ascetic and international Modern movement.

The emergence and ultimate success of Modernism, however, and its obsessions with technology and efficiency, disposed of the fireplace as a redundant technology, discarding it in favour of radiators or underfloor heating. Yet the fireplace survived in the suburbs. It remained central to the *idea* of home, and the house builders appreciated this – they were, after all, selling dreams of domesticity. In the 1930s, the mantelpiece gave way to a tiled, Art Deco surround, then to a gas heater fixed to the wall (perhaps with fake flames) subsequently topped with a mantelpiece. That, in turn, gave way to DIY repro-Victorian fireplaces, then to restored or reclaimed originals and finally to a theatrical minimalism. Interestingly, this trend has led to a revival of the firebowl as the centrepiece of the minimal modern hearth, an aesthetic that refers back to the original shallow bowls of the Greeks. The idea of the fireplace as architectural focus was, in time, reinvented as an essential part of every dwelling.

Its appeal is obvious. As the German observer Hermann Muthesius wrote in *The English House*, 'To an Englishman the idea of a room without a fireplace is quite simply unthinkable . . . the fireplace is the domestic altar before which daily and hourly he sacrifices to the household gods.'

The fireplace remains our domestic altar. Its archetype was dedicated to Vesta, but the later elaborate overmantels that supported clocks and urns now house anything from family photos or postcards from loved ones to tourist souvenirs and gewgaws and, perhaps most revealingly, large mirrors which reflect back the scenes of our everyday lives, as if we see our lives reflected above the flames. Like the massed fetishes Freud collected on his desk, these are symbols of a desire for meaning. They are our contemporary idols, representations of self, family, travel and the vague remnants of a once decorative art. The fireplace also becomes the site of celebration and ritual. Festive cards appear atop them: candles, garlands, holly, invitations and Christmas stockings. In their celebration of fire and the hearth they become the residing place of domestic Christmas. Even Santa Claus himself, the jolly spirit of midwinter and contemporary Dionysian plenty, emerges from the chimney in a strange manner vaguely redolent of Freudian notions.

In this way the fireplace represents a zone of communication with another world. When Magritte painted a suburban fireplace in *Time Transfixed*, he pictured a steam train emerging from it, its smoke rising back up the chimney. It exquisitely demonstrates the dreamlike strangeness of this realm of fire, air and darkness. For although the fireplace is the symbol of family and domesticity, it is far from unambiguous. Love letters are ritually tossed into the flames as lovers attempt to cleanse themselves of romantic misjudgements, or to destroy incriminating words. In *The Devil's Advocate*, the huge fireplace becomes a (rather too obvious) cipher for hell itself. Hitchcock's birds fly out of the fireplace in a representation of terrifying disruption, Truffaut's *Belle du Jour* casts her panties into the fireplace flames to discard, at least momentarily, her bourgeois conformity. The symbol of domesticity is also a place of turmoil and dreams, of passion and of the uncanny and the association with the furnace of cremation is hard to miss.

For the Romans the hearth represented the soul of the house and in our collective memory that meaning lives on. Radiators may well be more efficient but they have failed to capture our imagination in quite the same way. Surrounded by its domestic altar, the dark, smoke-blackened heart of the hearth resolutely remains the place where our domestic gods reside.

5   MOULDINGS

O NE OF THE MOST ELEGANT THINGS about architecture is the way in which ritual and symbolic elements transmute over time into practical features and then, once those practical uses too have been forgotten, hang around to haunt buildings as ghostly reminders of building's transmission from a vessel for worship to a place of dwelling.

The wall, like the column or like the classical temple, is divided into three parts, roughly corresponding to the base, the shaft and the capital of a column or, you could say, foundation, wall and roof. Now look at the way those parts are delineated in the architecture, in those 'original features'. There is the skirting board topped with a moulding, the wall and a picture rail, perhaps with a further moulding as the frieze above the picture rail hits the ceiling. The skirting board makes the transition from ground to wall, between the horizontal and the vertical. In symbolic terms this is the point at which the wall rises from the chaos of the earth and begins to impose the order of structure. It is usually topped with a simple moulding. The combinations of possible profiles for even the simplest of these are almost endless but there will usually be some kind of half round or quarter round detail and there is an entire and wonderfully rich vocabulary here for profiles; torus, scotia, astragal and so on. But fundamentally this is a foot. George Hersey, in his book *The Lost Meanings of Classical Architecture* (1988), suggests that each of these mouldings derives from the rituals of sacrifice in the Hellenic world. The temple was originally a place of sacrifice to the gods, each detail part of a hugely complex system of meaning and metaphor.

These lower mouldings, he says, represent the bound feet of a victim, perhaps human, perhaps animal, the round profile an echo of the rope (for which torus is another word). The scotia is the most interesting of these. Originally employed at the base of a Doric column, it is a concave moulding used to give shadow and visual weight to a base. We can see an echo of it in the slim shadow that runs the length of the skirting or below a projecting dado rail. The reason it is particularly interesting is that Scotia was the goddess of the underworld and of darkness and darkness was conceived not as we see it, as a lack of light, but as a physical substance, the shadow containing a miasma made black through a density of the tiny particles of dead souls.

Of course, the real reason for a skirting board was so that a floor could be mopped without damaging the plaster, so that it would be resistant to kicks and scuffs and easier to repaint when damaged without having to repaint the whole wall, but the mythical derivation survives. The dado is an interstitial moulding, one which derives from the point at which the timber panelling would have stopped and given way to the plaster wall, but it too has survived, as a mechanism for breaking up the monotony of the wall (and for protecting the wall from knocks with chair backs) it is, in effect, the waist of a room just as the skirting is its feet.

The picture rail and the frieze above it derive either from the capital of the column or from the frieze of a temple, they are the head of the room. Again there are an almost infinite number of variations of profiles, each giving a subtly different sense of shadow and mass. At its most elaborate it may meet the ceiling in a series of dentils, a row of cubic protrusions, which Hersey suggests (and their etymology supports) derive from the teeth which would have been used to ritually decorate horses. Another motif that occurs frequently is the curious egg and dart, the egg being a symbol of creation, of birth but also of the universe itself and an object used in sacrifice as its destruction is such a simple and symbolic act. Another, though far rarer, motif is composed of the skulls of oxen decorated with garlands, another memory of sacrifice in the temple. There was a moment in the explosion of Art Nouveau around 1900 when the frieze was suddenly resurrected as a realm of decoration: maidens and complex organic patterns were moulded into anaglypta, a mass-manufactured relief wallpaper made of wood pulp and cotton.

Practically, the picture rail represents the zone where the ceiling begins, the vault of the sky, and the point at which the paint changes from the wall to the ceiling finish. Again, the moulding marks the moment of structural transition. Moving across to the middle of the ceiling you may encounter a 'rose'. It may appear in a modern context as a surround for a lamp cable and you'd be forgiven for seeing it as a recent invention, but its history is intriguing. In Greek mythology Aphrodite, the goddess of love, gave her son Cupid a rose, which he in turn gave to the god of silence, Harpocrates, to ensure that his mother's sexual indiscretions would remain secret. Thus the rose became the symbol of domestic discretion. You may be familiar with the phrase 'sub-rosa' which derives from the Middle Ages, when a rose would be suspended above a council chamber ensuring that the occupants would be sworn to secrecy once outside.

There is an assumption that Modernism wiped away all these symbolic devices, but in fact you could argue their memory survived. Minimalist designers continue to employ what they now call 'shadow gaps' between surfaces – dark channels which distinguish wall surfaces from floors or from doors. What are these if not the inheritors of the scotia? We continue to build our houses on the souls of our ancestors.

6

BOOKS

BOOKS ARE, LIKE BRICKS, a basic element of architecture. I wasn't quite aware of this myself until I viewed a couple of properties recently and was struck, and appalled, by the lack of books inside. No books. Not one. The interiors, otherwise impeccably over-designed, seemed painfully incomplete. Bereft.

At the exact moment that the book would seem to be in the greatest danger in its history, threatened by e-books and a proliferation of the disposable technical gadgets complete with built-in obsolescence, the book's very old technology seems at its most attractive – and its most physical. E-readers may be able to convey content but they leave no physical trace. Once the machine is turned off or fails, the knowledge disappears. They are resolutely not a part of the architecture but rather of the increasingly messy landscape of stuff. Libraries and bookstacks have always been a physical and aesthetic manifestation of knowledge, of the world informed by reading and, consequently, a way of reading the inhabitant. There is more information to be gleaned about the occupant of a house from what is on the shelves than from the furniture or the food. Books – or the lack of them – form an almost perfect mirror of concerns and character.

As well as being a means of expression – whether conscious or unconscious – books serve another representational purpose.

From the Renaissance – and on through the Enlightenment and into a world in which books went from being precious, handmade treasures to affordable commodities – the library or the study lined with books was a cipher for an ordered reality, a defence against a real world outside that could be frighteningly unpredictable. Within their pages lay the answers, the knowledge to fend off an apparent lack of meaning in the universe. Yet, paradoxically, in their disorder, in the random systems we impose (or fail to impose) upon them, they can equally represent the impossibility of knowing. The German thinker Walter Benjamin, in his beautiful essay 'Unpacking my Library', managed to reconcile these ideas whilst contemplating his books as yet unpacked but in a new apartment: 'the chance, the fate that suffuse the past before my eyes are conspicuously present in the accustomed confusion of these books. For what else is this collection but a disorder to which habit has accommodated itself to such an extent that it can appear as order?' Georges Perec makes a similar point in considering his shelves: 'We would like to think,' he writes 'that order and disorder are in fact the same word, denoting pure chance.' The library can also denote the end of time. To find someone's library in a second-hand bookshop is an extraordinarily moving thing, a document of a life abruptly ended at the moment acquisition stops. But it can be voluntary. There was Jules Verne's Captain Nemo, who built a private library in his submarine; 12,000 uniformly bound volumes submerged with him, the sum of all knowledge up to the point at which, for him, it all stopped, there would be nothing new.

A wall covered in spines, shelved from floor to ceiling, recognizes the correspondence between bricks and books. It is the point at which knowledge becomes embedded in structure and the appearance is of books holding up the ceiling. The implication is that enlightenment, the journey towards the sky or the sublime is available within these pages. It is a metaphor made clearer by the special pieces of furniture, the chairs and stools which ingeniously convert to become ladders or in the sliding steps which glide along the floor scanning the shelves. And just as bricks humanize the scale of even a vast wall by introducing an element of human scale – a solid unit designed to fit perfectly into the hand, so books define the space and give scale to even the largest wall. They are endlessly reproduced and faked in a game of *trompe l'oeil* in which their symbolic role alone is invoked. There are bookish wallpapers, there are rows of fake book spines, there are hidden jib doors hidden among the bookshelves which open, just as books do themselves, to reveal another world, and there are dealers who specialize in slightly-worn, leather-spined books by the yard, not for reading but for recreating a country house effect, the impression of history and wisdom. Already in the first century AD Seneca swore by a small library, for knowledge rather than vanity, not 'endless bookshelves for the ignorant to decorate their dining rooms.'

Just as bricks can be laid in a panoply of bonds, so books can be built into aesthetic systems. I am always a little annoyed when I see books ordered by the colour of the spine, but it is inevitable we order them by size according to the heights of the shelves – a system which can do terrible things to the logic of what goes where – but also produce delightful serendipities; my oversize shelf sees Will Eisner next to *The Cold War*, *Graphics for Signage* between *The Wonder Book of Inventions* and *Fairground Art*. There are alphabetical and chronological possibilities, ordering by language and theme or, for the ambitious, the Dewey Decimal. Samuel Pepys abhorred irregularity and had little platform soles made of wood to place beneath shorter volumes so the whole row would reach the same height. But putting books in order gives the reader the chance to become an architect, to build a personal world in which, almost certainly, only the user has the key to understanding the order, to travelling through the words.

And then, there is the possibility that order breaks down completely. From an architectural point of view, this is paradoxically the moment of chaos when books become not a representation of structure but the structure itself – piled up on the floor, on shelves, above shelves, on tables and chairs, blocking out windows until the room disappears. The ultimate architecture of books was built by Patrice Moore, a Bronx resident who was found, barely alive, in his single small room under an avalanche of books and papers into which he had carved a tiny corner in which to sleep. Moore recalls the urban legend that was Homer and Langley Collyer, similarly consumed within their own papers in a Harlem brownstone, their extraordinary lives commemorated and fictionalized in E.L. Doctorow's *Homer & Langley*. To these New Yorkers, a world constructed of books and paper had become both heaven and hell, a self-constructed world both escape and confinement. Homer became blind, inhabiting the trenches within the house like a mole. Jorge Luis Borges too, went blind but saw a world of books as heaven. 'I have always imagined,' he wrote, 'that paradise will be a kind of library,' and, indeed, he opens his haunting story 'The Library of Babel' with the words 'The Universe (which others call the Library)'.

But it is Benjamin again, unpacking his books, 'not yet touched by the mild boredom of order', who writes most eloquently about the edifice constructed by the reader from words and how they will ultimately, and pleasurably consume him. It is 'Not that they [the books] come alive in him,' he writes, 'it is he who comes alive in them. So I have erected one of his dwellings, with books as the building stones, before you, and now he is going to disappear inside, as is only fitting.'

7 DINING ROOMS

THE DINING ROOM IS BOTH absolutely pivotal to the idea of the bourgeois dwelling and simultaneously completely dispensable. There is no need for a dining room. We can eat in kitchens or in living rooms, in our beds, on the floor or watching TV with trays perched on our laps or on inadequate tables. So the dining room is really all about show, about a display. Its importance to bourgeois culture is highlighted by its persistent presence in parodies of middle class life, in satire and surrealism, in art and caricature.

The dinner party is the ultimate object of derision for radical artists, the symbol of the middle class obsession with status, self-image and domestic pride. Louis Buñuel's *The Discreet Charm of the Bourgeoisie* sees guests unbuttoning their trousers and hitching up their skirts to sit down for dinner on toilet bowls. They then retire alone to a small locked room served by a dumb waiter to eat lunch by themselves in privacy. The dining room as the *de facto* space of bourgeois manners is satirized in Francis Weber's *Le Diner de Cons*, a French farce in which guests challenge each other to bring the biggest idiot to dinner. If our dining traditions are based on those of the French (the English couldn't even be bothered to develop a vocabulary of fine dining), then it is also the French who have parodied their own traditions most mercilessly.

Nowhere is this clearer than in Marco Ferreri's *La Grande Bouffe* (1973), in which a party of men decide to eat and drink themselves to death in the company of prostitutes, so that sex and excess and food are all mixed up in a fatal theatricality, the laden dining table becoming the surface for sex, dining and death. This is a role loaded with religious symbolism. The altar is the archetype of the ritual table and each dining table carries within it the memory – no matter how faint – of the altar. Its symbolism is threefold. First there is the sacrificial altar. From the Old Testament tradition, a blood sacrifice was made upon the altar to cleanse worshippers of their sins. In the Christian Mass this developed into the communion, in which worshippers drink and eat the transubstantiated blood and flesh of their saviour. On the dining room table, you could argue, the dignity and respect with which a joint or a fowl is carved is an echo of this role. The second symbolic role is that of the sarcophagus, the tomb for Christ. When the early Christians worshipped they were forced to do so underground, in the catacombs of Rome. Their early altars were the stone tombs of their ancestors. It isn't done much any more, but the laying of the coffin out on the dining table for a wake or vigil is the contemporary equivalent to this idea. Finally the table represents the place at which Christ and his disciples sat at the Last Supper. Every still life in art, every mafia film showing a family around a table eating spaghetti, and every banquet bears the traces and the memories of this meal. It is a place of family and friends but also of betrayal and death. The Flemish and Spanish still lifes of seventeenth century depict tables with crumpled cloths and half-drunk glasses of wine, in which fruit is beginning to rot and silver platters sit precariously over the edge of the table. These are *memento mori*, reminders of the short time we have on earth.

Of course any old surface can become a dining table if you eat off it: a coffee table, a crate, a breakfast bar, the arm of a sofa. But it is only when a cloth is laid upon a surface that it is dedicated, designated as such. It is surely the easiest act of transformation from the quotidian to the special. In Frank Capra's *It's a Wonderful Life*, the newlyweds, forced to abandon their honeymoon, are given a meal by their friends who transform a room in the still-derelict house of their dreams into a dining room through the addition of a gingham tablecloth and a candlestick. That's all it takes.

At the other end of the scale, of course, the dining room was the representative space, the room of theatre and entertainment. Food was once associated with luxury. The more, the richer. Consequently the dining room became an event space. When the Prince Regent built himself a country house by the sea at Brighton in 1787, he employed the architect John Nash to create an extraordinary explosion of exoticism. A clash of Mughal indulgence and spectacular orientalism, it was an absurd indulgence but one which perfectly illustrates the theatricality of event dining. The walls were decorated with Chinoiserie, the columns terminate in sculpted palm leaves and a great dragon coils around the rose above a huge chandelier. This is the kind of aesthetic that Peter York calls 'Dictator Chic' (though 200 years early) – the overblown kitsch that characterizes the frustration of the Regent or the insecurity of the leader who needs to establish himself through decoration. It is the aesthetic expression of the man who wants more. Greed.

That kind of decorative inflation though can also lead to ennui. The space becomes a symptom of boredom. In *Citizen Kane* we see the plutocrat each morning at breakfast dining at the table with the company of a newspaper despite his increasingly disaffected wife sitting opposite. The scene is repeated in Michel Hazanavicius's *The Artist*, the dining table becoming a scene of frustration and numbing repetition, of disaffection with married life. But these are breakfasts, perhaps taking place somewhere rather different to the more formal dining room.

Few of us now have breakfast rooms but it was once quite the thing. Sir John Soane's breakfast room at his Lincoln's Inn Fields house is one of the happiest places in a dark, brooding house. Small and intimate – its edges lined with bookcases and by light flooding in from above – it has a centre defined by a shallow dome suspended above it, which delineates the dining area in the same way that a tablecloth creates and defines a surface for dining. Breakfast is not only at the opposite end of the day to dinner, it is also the architectural counterpoint to the dining room. Breakfast is private. The couple are not on display but at ease around a small table just big enough for a tray of tea and toast. Its position in the house has been supplanted by the kitchen and by the increasing speed of breakfast which now tends to be a quick bowl of cereal, if anything at all. It is barely considered a meal. The radical changes in dining habits present an extremely interesting dilemma to the symbolic aspects of the home. The dining room is central to an idea of hospitality, and the word 'host' means one who offers hospitality (the root is the same for both 'hospital' and 'hotel') – not to offer that hospitality is to be 'hostile', to deliberately alienate. (Incidentally the word 'ghost' derives from *ghosti* or stranger – the one to whom you must show hospitality.)

If the dining space is the built representation of family and friendship, of hospitality, then its elimination is a deliberate and politically symbolic gesture. That is precisely what happened in the apartments built during the early Modernist and Communist eras across Europe and particularly in the Soviet Bloc. The Modernists attempted to encourage communal dining, to dispense as far as possible with kitchens and dining rooms in apartments. Grete Shütte-Lihotsky's Frankfurt kitchen, which became ubiquitous in German social housing between the wars, is an ingenious design for a minimal kitchen, often credited as the most important contribution by a woman to the Bauhaus era. Yet the irony is that Shütte-Lihotsky's design effectively marginalized women into a small cabin, disconnected from the rest of the family (the room was too small to have children running in and out) and geared towards a Taylorist idea of cooking as production: an activity to be made more efficient rather than more enjoyable. The architects of the Communist era took this idea and amplified it, squeezing the kitchen till it squeaked and disposing with the dining room altogether. One interpretation of this move (apart from the obvious space-saving aspect) was that it suited the regime well to discourage family togetherness and the company of friends. The one thing that stood in the way of the State's complete control of the individual was family loyalty. It is a moot point whether Soviet architects and their Eastern European comrades were instructed to minimize dining space for this reason, but it certainly happened. Kitchens were big enough to accommodate a table for two or three at most. Living rooms, once stuffed with a sofabed, TV and obligatory vitrine, were too small for a dining table and chairs and the result was the desired atomization of family life. The same result has been achieved in the West through the TV dinner. Dining rooms are a politically as well as a symbolically charged space.

8

KITCHENS

THE MODERN KITCHEN IS VERY MUCH the heart of the home. It has become the default contemporary social space, a place of both intimate family meals and of informal social intercourse. Yet barely a century ago, the kitchen languished as a marginal place, populated only by servants or the poor.

The story of domestic architecture is one of the trickle down effect from the mansions and palaces of the nobility down through the bourgeoisie and, finally, the labouring classes. Yet the story of the kitchen's emergence as the heart of the contemporary dwelling is an exception to the rule – it trickles up.

The kitchen today is the cockpit of the dwelling, its high-tech gadgets and stainless steel fittings and electronics confirm its status as the nerve centre. Not-yet-built apartments are sold on the basis of upmarket kitchen specifications and pictures of expensive-looking, restaurant-quality cookers and fittings, rich marble work surfaces and fitted cabinetry. It is the only part of the house that has succumbed to the seductive world of fashion-style branding: Poggenpohl, Smeg, Aga, Bosch or Bulthaup are worn like Prada, Barbour or Boss. Far from being hidden downstairs or in a blocky back extension, it is now often found as an accessory to the main room, a status symbol opened through into the living room or at the heart of a big, single 'entertaining space'. In the Anglo Saxon world at least, the greatest paradox is that as the kitchen becomes ever more visible and visibly expensive, its actual use is declining. The most functional of domestic spaces has become a symbol.

The kitchen's story begins outside the grand medieval house: a separate block-house, the fire and fumes of which were regarded as dangerous and noxious. The widespread adoption of the chimney, as late as the end of the sixteenth century, brought the kitchen into the home, yet kept at the back of the house, in the realm of the servants. Solidly built, with the hearth at its heart (the warmest place in the house), and busy, it functioned as the engine of the everyday but its separateness did not mean it could not be a grand space. From the huge halls of Hampton Court to the Arts and Crafts solidity of Lutyens' monumental Castle Drogo, it could feature among the most impressive rooms in the house even if the owners themselves probably never entered it.

The scale and extent of the kitchens in a grand house is difficult to comprehend today. In a country house, where the family might only be present for a few months a year or a couple of seasons, food would need to be stored and processed in huge quantities through the year. There were endless warrens of rooms associated with all these processes. There would be a scullery and a bakehouse, perhaps a pastry room, game larder or avenary, buttery, a sauce room, a napery (for storing linen), rooms for cleaning and storing cutlery (which was all silver and needed to be polished), knife rooms (these needed to be sharpened and oiled or greased to stop them rusting), a dairy, a still (for brewing and distilling spirits for drinking or cleaning) and perhaps a room for the huge retinue of servants themselves to eat in. Half the volume of a house by plan area might be taken up with service spaces, but these were rooms that would never have been entered by members of the family, who would have very little contact with many of those below and very little idea about what went on.

In working class households, however, the kitchen was everything. In tenements and back-to-backs, the kitchen was bathroom, bedroom, living room and dining room, with a tin bath and often an alcove for sleeping. It symbolized home and hospitality, an urn hanging above a fire for tea and toast on tap, a crude timber table serving as the dwelling's public piazza. A kitchen range might combine the functions of hearth, over, cooker and hot water heater. It was almost like a steam engine pumping energy from the centre of the dwelling.

The biggest change in the conception of kitchens came when the middle classes began to lose their servants, when labour became too expensive – though it suddenly became apparent exactly how much hard physical labour was involved in feeding a family.

The kitchen became the realm of the housewife not the housekeeper. At first, in the Edwardian era, it remained physically distinct, a simple space in the basement. Even in fairly modest houses and apartments kitchens would have been supplemented by a scullery and a larder or pantry. The acts of washing up and cooking were separated out, cooking in the kitchen and washing up in the scullery (the word derives from the French *escuelle* – dishes) and storage in the larder (from the Old French *lardier* or a place for the storage of salted meats, the same root as for 'lard' or 'lardons') or pantry (from the Old French *paneterie* or bread room).

Modernism was, initially at least, unkind to the kitchen. Taylorist ideas of efficiency were translated in the US and in Germany into a new functional idea of the kitchen which aspired to the aesthetic of a laboratory. Margarete Schütte-Lihotsky conceived food preparation as a necessary chore, to be carried out alone and made as efficient and hygienic as possible. Fold-down surfaces and fitted storage in which everything had its place depersonalized the vagaries and eccentricities of kitchens and made them minimal cells. Pleasure in process or consumption was equally efficiently extracted.

In the US, meanwhile, the kitchen became a status symbol, the technological hub of the house in which housewives proudly displayed their washers, dryers, blenders, toasters, juicers and coffee makers. The kitchen was used as a site of consumption, part of a US policy of absorbing the huge Post-War economic surplus. The nation had done well out of the war, its military industrial complex – by now by far the biggest in the world – had adapted well to the production of military hardware and now it needed to adapt back. The outlet became the kitchen – the room in which a succession of gadgets kept folk spending and kept factories busy producing new, improved machines. Labour-saving devices from washers and dryers, dishwashers, blenders, juicers, coffee grinders and percolators, electric kettles and kitchen knives, bread makers, chip fryers, ice makers and ice cream makers, fridges, freezers, microwaves, pressure cookers and toasters – no other room in the house is so in thrall to technology and the consumption driven by these new devices (and their planned obsolescence) fed US and European Post War growth as they fed their users.

These changes in technology were at least in part driven by the increasing expense of domestic staff. The paradox between the homely and the high-tech remains at the heart of the kitchen but the proliferation of stainless steel surfaces and racks of tools, of microwaves and mixers does recall one of the most fundamental archetypes, the idea of alchemy. The kitchen is psychologically linked to the idea of miraculous transformation, of the manufacture of seductive food from base materials. It is the place in the house where the elements come together, the fruits of the earth, fire, water and air (or gas). In symbolic terms it is the place of miracles as well as that most closely associated with the mother and domesticity itself.

Those miracles are made visible through the increasing perception of the kitchen as a place of performance and domestic theatre. The contemporary continuous kitchen/dining/living space privileges the act of food preparation and cooking and can be interpreted as an attempt to give women a role in the everyday drama of domestic life commensurate with their pivotal role in running the household. Cooking is reinterpreted as a creative act (which is why men too become suddenly more interested in domestic cooking). Henri Lefebvre in fact interpreted the explosion in the number of gadgets and machines as a legitimization of consumption and modernity through association with the archetypal demands of food and domesticity.

The kitchen is defined not so much by its space as by its contents, from faux-farmhouse to molecular laboratory and every point between. The more the traditional family is fragmented, the less food we actually cook, the more the kitchen becomes a cipher for the half-remembered world we think we have lost or the fantasy lifestyle we desire. Few kitchens, even in France, bear even traces of Proust's remembered madeleines, but they can evoke them in other ways, through style or through vintage fittings and furniture, through an idea of 'kitchenness'.

For all our use of the home as a status symbol or a version of ourselves, few of us actually exert much control over the architecture of where we live. We choose stuff from catalogues or websites, our taste is dictated by the available or the existing (if we move into a newly-built or renovated home), it is a kind of pick 'n' mix design.

Consequently the kitchen, where we in fact have a broader range of themes and memories to choose from and to evoke, becomes a surrogate, the clearest indicator of real taste and aspiration, if only rarely, ironically, of the way life is actually lived.

9

'WE DON'T THINK ENOUGH ABOUT STAIRCASES,' the writer Georges Perec once opined. 'Nothing was more beautiful in old houses than the staircases. Nothing is uglier, colder, more hostile, meaner, in today's apartment buildings. We should learn to live more on staircases. But how?'

How, indeed. Stairs are perhaps the most obviously symbolic of architectural elements and their meaning the most easily interpreted. They are about the ascent to a higher realm, literally and metaphorically.

The dwelling in the classical world was generally single-storey. Even the grandest Roman villas tended to be arranged on a single floor. So stairs were associated solely with the temple, with the gods. The hieroglyph for the Egyptian god of resurrection and the afterlife, Osiris, was always preceded by a stair. Every religion places its structures atop steps. Many of the temple structures themselves are an embodiment of the stairs to the heavens, whether in the stepped profiles of Egyptian or Meso-American pyramids or of Buddhist stupas. Greek and Roman temples are reached by steps. Then there was the church, the steps to its door and the raising of the sanctuary and the Holy of Holies as well as the endless spiralling stairs to its belfry or its spire.

As houses became grander and taller, roughly from the Renaissance, this symbolism of ascent immediately became a moment of architectural theatre. The main entertaining level, the piano nobile, was lifted up to an expansive first floor, which left the ground floor as, essentially, a space for containing the stairs. Situated at the heart of the structure, the only available light was from above; rooflights and lanterns illuminated the stairs so that you ascended towards the light – the perfect metaphor.

In the nineteenth century the emergence of the opera house, with its grand stair, denoted a high point in the image of steps as theatrical motif; these were social staircases upon which to pose, to appear. This form of very public showing-off then fed directly back into domestic architecture. From *Gone with the Wind* to *Double Indemnity*, the *grande dame* and the *femme fatale* appear at the top of the stairs as if by magic, like an apparition of beauty, looking down from above on the suddenly besotted man, forcing him to crane his neck, to put her on a pedestal.

Freud, of course, associated stairs with sex. 'Steps, ladders or staircases,' he wrote 'or, as the case may be, walking up or down them, are representations of the sexual act.'

It is a controversial idea but one deeply, if subconsciously, engrained in both popular and high culture. The word *climax*, it is worth noting, was ancient Greek for 'ladder'. Stairs are physically demanding and they can take your breath away, metaphorically as well as actually. For Carl Jung, however, the stairs represented something else, the movement from the subconscious to the conscious mind. Jung saw the house as a representation of the self and the floors as the levels of the human sub-conscious. Slavoj Žižek sees the famous house in Alfred Hithcock's *Psycho* as the perfect illustration of this idea. The three levels on which the action takes place, Žižek suggests, correspond to the three levels of human subjectivity. The ground floor represents the ego, where Norman Bates acts out the everyday existence of son and motel keeper. The first floor, the realm of the dead mother, represents the super ego, and the cellar corresponds to the id, the reservoir of his illicit sex drive. Thus, when Bates carries the skeletal remains of his mother from the first floor to the cellar, he is symbolically transposing her from super ego to id, illustrating the intimate link between the two components.

The stairs also represent, in a strange house at least, an ascent – or descent - into an unknown realm. A grand stair rarely rises straight up; it usually involves a landing, mezzanine or dog-leg so that the destination is hidden. That landing provides the critical pause, the stage upon which everything is revealed: status, wealth, beauty but also destination and destiny.

Look at how the film noir *femme fatale* sensuously runs her elegant fingers along the handrail, or at Nosferatu's bony fingers as they are silhouetted against the balustrade. This also reminds us that the stairs represent the first moment of physical engagement with the architecture. The door would have been opened by a maid or footman, so the handrail is left as possibly the only time you touch a part of the house, fingers caressing it, sliding up and down. The balusters that terminate the handrail are nearly always suitably phallic.

Marcel Duchamp's 1912 painting *Nude Descending a Staircase* explicitly denies the sensuality of this most historically sexualized architectural element in his stripping of the sensuous nude into a series of fractured angles, while also introducing a new conception of movement through space and time. In the early years of Modernism the staircase and its close cousin, the ramp, were often at the heart of the new architecture, the symbolism of ascending to the light perfectly in tune with the search for a new beginning.

Modernist architects sought to reduce the stair, as the Georgians had before them, to a minimal structure. While their eighteenth-century forebears cantilevered slender stone steps from the wall to produce an effect of weightlessness, the denial of the substance of the stone treads, the Modernists created staircases of fragility and transparency. This translucence, the use of glass and perforated metal, of floating stairs, was an interesting attempt to reduce a less desirable aspect of the structure, the idea that something might be lurking beneath it, or at its top.

The strange, liminal space below the stairs and the dark negative of the steps to the cellar below (the cellar steps appear as a sinister shadow version of the formal steps above them, stripped of all detail and beauty – skeleton stairs) are familiar hiding places for the imagined nasties of childhood. Most of us will be familiar with the sinister feeling of being followed up darkened stairs at night. I certainly used to bound up the stairs in my childhood house in the dark for fear of an unknown, unseen pursuer. Robert Mitchum's terrifying psychopath calling to the children from the top of the stairs in *The Night of the Hunter* beautifully captures this kind of evil presence.

Often underplayed is the role of the stair as a social hub. In offices, landings produce creative social encounters and buildings for universities, for labs and offices are now routinely designed so that the stairs are generous public spaces that encourage encounter. It was to this that Perec was referring, particularly in the apartment block, where the stairs were the place of random meetings, everyday conversations and fond goodbyes. Within the dwelling, the stairs have become a simple ascending corridor, stripped of their role as a place of communication and lingering. The rich, it is interesting to note, still demand grand stairs. From McMansions via neo-Georgian country houses to Russian dachas, the theatrical staircase remains de rigueur, the purest symbol of social climbing.

10 CELLARS & ATTICS

THE CELLAR, WRITES GASTON BACHELARD, 'is first and foremost the dark entity of the house, the one that partakes of subterranean forces. When we dream there, we are in harmony with the irrationality of the depths.'

Bachelard's beautiful book, a keystone of phenomenology, *The Poetics of Space* (1958), proposes the house as a representation of both mind and body, its feet firmly on the ground, its roof aspiring to the verticality of Man against the horizontality of the landscape. Thus, the attic is seen as the space of reflection, 'Up near the roof,' he writes, 'all our thoughts are clear'. It is the tower, reaching for the clouds while protecting the inhabitants from them.

Freud, too, saw the cellar as the receptacle of the subconscious. But it frankly doesn't take a psychiatrist or a phenomenologist to understand the cellar and the attic as the twin representatives of memory and half-forgotten dreams. These are dark places, unfinished, lacking the workmanship of the other rooms of the house, indicating that these rooms are not places for habitation. The cellar and the garret are instead places of the unformed image. They are where we store the relics of our past, the now-unused items to which we remain attached, warehouses of memory and neglect.

But this is not just sentiment. As Bachelard suggests, these twin architectural poles are also bastions of the sinister, the deliberately buried or forgotten. Whether in the image of the mad Mrs Rochester shut away in the attic or in the terrifying nightmare reality of Joseph Fritzl's basement dungeon (which chillingly reminds us of the etymology of the 'cellar' as a collection of cells), the idea of the basement and the attic also embodies a terrible notion of the imprisonment of the unwanted, both symbolic and actual. The basement is, in its way, the domestic version of the cemetery, an underground realm of darkness and mystery. From mass murderers who bury their victims beneath the basement floor to images of boilers and coal cellars that speak of the dark heat of hell, these are the lairs of horror and the gothic imagination. Countless films feature the terror in the cellar; it represents the unknown. The Latin *celare* implies keeping something secret – it is related to the word 'conceal'. The cellar is the cave, the elemental realm below. The Germanic words *Höhle* (cave) and *Holle* (Hell) are intimately related, and we still retain the coal holes that indicate the blackness below. In the 1927 film *Metropolis*, Fritz Lang shows us a future world of proles and drudges existing in an underground system of caverns whilst their bourgeois brethren frolic in the penthouses above.

Perhaps the best evocation of the strange terror of the cellar appears in Jan Švankmajer's short film *Down to the Cellar* (1983). Here, seen through the eyes of a little girl, a journey down to the cellar of an apartment block becomes an odyssey, fraught with terror and surprise. This, the director makes clear, is a realm of the strange and the uncanny. The little girl's task is simple: she must descend the rickety stairs to bring up a basket of potatoes. But her task is confronted by endless, surreal obstacles. A strange old man goes to bed in his pyjamas and covers himself with a blanket of coal; an aproned lady bakes cakes from coaldust; the rough-sawn, quartered logs ready for stoves upstairs beat the girl around the head and the potatoes don't want to go. They roll out of her basket back in their box, reluctant to leave their subterranean realm of darkness. Things down here like the dark. The black cat totem follows the girl around, guarding the shadow below the house. The potatoes remind us that the cellar is the realm in which root vegetables were stored in old farmhouses – dark, dank, replicating the conditions of the underground. It is the root of the dwelling.

We get another creepy communal basement in Roman Polanski's *Rosemary's Baby* (1968). Mia Farrow's character harbours a fear of the space and agrees to do her laundry with another girl she meets down there so neither has to be below ground alone. Her new friend is then found dead on the ground in front of the building. The same trope appears in *Home Alone*: the basement houses a boiler that seems to roar into life. Cellars are there to scare kids.

The fear and potency of this psychically charged subterranean world would be revealed in the efforts of the Modernists to rid architecture of the dark recesses of the house. A year after the release of *Metropolis*, Le Corbusier designed the Villa Savoye, a house elevated above the ground on slender structural columns (which he called *piloti*, a word resonant of the airborne, of pilots) which exemplifies the efforts to detach architecture from the underground. It is removed from the earth, floating above it in a clear denunciation of the idea of a visceral engagement with the subterranean. This is a house of lightness, both in weight and illumination. There will be no darkness in the crystal clear architecture of Modernism. It was not just Corbusier: Mies van der Rohe's Farnsworth House and Philip Johnson's Glass House are exemplars of the urge to disengage with the ground, to avoid Freud's void. Frank Lloyd Wright, too, despite his ideas of organic engagement with the landscape, wrote of two essential housing archetypes: the cave and the tent. The cave is a cipher for the old world – dark, primitive, subterranean, stuck – the tent stands for the new world – mobile, at home in any landscape, light on its feet. The cave is the house with a cellar, the tent is a Modernist villa sitting lightly on the landscape.

The garret, though, is less of a lost cause. The lofty space of raw rafters and dusty joists is gradually disappearing in a frenzy of conversions, Velux windows and en suites, as the roof void gives way to au-pair accommodation and guest rooms. It is a move that echoes the status of the garret as servant's accommodation or usefully leftover space. This, remember, is the realm of *La Bohème*. The idea of the capacious loft space appropriated by artists has come to mean expansive, abandoned industrial space, but its roots lie in the large roofspaces of big apartment buildings, which artists made their own in bohemian Paris and New York. These were spaces ideal for appropriation, close to the sky, often brightly lit as they are not shaded by the buildings opposite, where life could be lived away from the bourgeois preoccupations of the street and the courtyard.

The cellar and the loft are the mythical realms of the house, its labyrinth and its heavens. Both cellars and attics, in their neglect and their darkness, engage with time, with dust and decay and with the past and the subconscious. They are the domestic conduits of memory.

11 BEDROOMS

It all begins on the bed. Perhaps our tenderest and perhaps our most ecstatic moments occur there and, if we're lucky, perhaps it all ends there too. We may no longer be born or die in our own bedrooms, instead emerging and expiring under the sickly flickering fluorescents of the hospital, but we are probably still conceived in the bedroom and, of all the rooms in our house, it remains the most intimate, the most private and the most precious. It is the room in which you are most vulnerable, asleep and unaware, the room in which you dream. The displays of family photos, the mementoes, cuddly toys, the jewellery and candles all point to an intimacy, an idea of the bedroom as an inner sanctum.

But it wasn't always this way. The bedroom is, in architectural terms, an archaeological revival. The wealthier Romans might have had a cubiculum, a small private chamber for sleeping and retreat (from *cubo*, 'to lie down', which is also where we get the word 'cubicle' from) and the same name was given to the niche in an early Christian catacomb church (sleeping, sex and death are always unsettlingly close) but the custom died out for over a thousand years after their empire collapsed. English houses of the medieval period disdained privacy. There might be a raised dais or platform for the head of the house and his immediate family to sleep above the level of the animals and workers who shared his house (which would keep them above the layer of animal shit), but probably not much more. Bigger, richer houses though might have featured a 'solar'. This was nothing to do with the sun, as its etymology might suggest, but rather derived from the French word *seule* or 'alone'. Situated on the upper level of the house, this was a small chamber for withdrawing, perhaps engaging in solitary activity – reading, embroidery, intimate conversation or making love. But it may not have been where the head of the household slept; rather, it was a kind of parlour because the kind of bedroom intimacy we have come to expect had not quite been invented yet. Sleeping, like almost every other aspect of life, was a communal activity and one which, particularly during the long nights of winter, may have involved several sessions, interrupted by wakefulness and conversation, perhaps again, sex, and then a bit more sleep.

Even for the wealthiest (in fact especially for the wealthiest), the bedroom was a semi-public space, a room of display and for receiving guests rather than withdrawing. The wonderful Great Bed of Ware (which can be seen in London's Victoria & Albert Museum), carved around the end of the sixteenth century, could sleep up to fifteen. All in perfect privacy.

For Louis XIV, the bedroom was the centre of royal ritual with Versailles' swarms of courtiers flocking to his waking and lying down, the strange ceremonies of the 'Lever' and the 'Coucher'. The Sun King rose and set like the golden orb that was his symbol and, as if in homage to some ancient pagan rite, he was worshipped. Kings all over Europe received their guests in their bedchambers, often on their beds. The only privacy to be had was by turning the bed itself into a room, thus the four-poster surrounded by curtains, a room within a room, also an effective way of excluding draughts in underheated rooms. Rembrandt's etching *The Bed* shows a canopy draped above the bed creating a kind of tent within which to make love. Its shelter becomes a microcosm, a room within a room. Similarly his *Young Woman in Bed*, with the girl holding the curtain back, suggests a theatrically separate world.

Another Rembrandt, *Interior with Saskia in Bed*, shows a more modest bed, carved into the wall of the house, a place of withdrawing into the very fabric of the wall. Dutch beds of this era became cupboards with curtains – dark, insulated architectural spaces rather than pieces of furniture. The style of living and of the house usually emerges from the palace and trickles down to more modest dwellings, but the notion of privacy travelled the other way. It was the emerging bourgeoisie in Holland, then England, who built houses with smaller, more private bedrooms, and royalty followed.

Elsewhere, beds were more communal. Poorer families would sleep together and guests would often join them. There weren't the same taboos as there are today about sleeping together, although there would probably have been a fixed hierarchy in who slept where, unmarried daughters sleeping apart from strangers and guests with the couple lying together in the middle of the bed to keep them apart.

Louis XIV's Versailles represented the other end of the spectrum – the zenith of the public bed – but it was his successor Louis XV's rather bourgeois one-time mistress Madame de Pompadour who brought something approaching the modern bedroom into the palace. She had a passion for interior decoration, persistently building and decorating little houses around the vast, sprawling complex of Versailles. Their rooms included boudoirs and bedrooms, modest, intimate spaces decorated in the delicate style known as Rococo – which she was at least partly responsible for making the default style of eighteenth century France and, consequently, most of Europe. These first bedrooms were already feminized in style, their walls richly decorated with shells and scrolls, gilded lilies and exotic wallpapers. Privacy was required for dignity, it wouldn't have done for the queen to walk in on the king in the act with another, so separate bedrooms were built, often connected by secret passages and long galleries.

There were also boudoirs, which similarly emerged in the eighteenth century. The word emerges from the French *bouder*, to sulk. These were smaller rooms off the bedrooms and off the public circuit of the enfilade (the grand procession of rooms each opening one into the other to create a theatrical architectural vista) for ladies to withdraw into a more private realm.

These rooms then emerged from sex but were, in their way, expressions of female taste. Arguably this remains the case. If the living room is dominated by high-tech expressions of wealth, consumption and entertainment – the latest TVs or Hi-Fis, the big paintings, grand fireplaces and sofas which exemplify a male idea of status – the bedroom remains the intimate realm of the woman. Freud in fact associates it exclusively with the female, with the wife. If Madame de Pompadour popularized the idea of the delicately decorated bedroom as the privileged space of sex, the Hollywood films of the 1930s revivified the idea. After years of being hidden away, of being an increasingly private space, the movies brought the bedroom back into public view.

The movies became the fantasy of desire, sexual and material. To paraphrase Slavoj Žižek, they not only told us what to desire but *how* to desire. Women swooned over Rudolf Valentino but they also noted the backgrounds against which the drama played, the satin drapes and exotic materials, the round mirrors and matching dressing room sets. In the first flush of the movies in the late 1920s and early 1930s (before the strict Hays codes were introduced to govern the screen portrayal of intimacy) the bedroom appeared as the luscious, glamorous backdrop for stars in their silk nightgowns and satin robes. Dashing, pencil-moustachioed set designer Cedric Gibbons, the most prolific and flamboyant of the movie bedroom designers, became a kind of star himself, married to sultry sex symbol Dolores del Rio. His sumptuous bedroom designs featured huge stepped mirrors, silk drapes, geometric furniture, animal skin rugs and beds with Art Deco headboards as big as the film screen itself. Even hapless Laurel and Hardy's wives dwelt in Hollywood-glam bedrooms. In Otto Preminger's 1944 film *Laura*, we see the detective investigating the (supposed) murder of the eponymous character wandering around her apartment, rifling through her underwear and her personal effects and falling in love. He falls asleep below her portrait and wakes up to find her alive and present. The bedroom has become a cipher for femininity, so strong that it has seemingly resurrected her.

As Hollywood's moral codes became more prohibitive, subsequent movie bedrooms would be less visible. Certainly there were the bedroom farces of Doris Day and Rock Hudson, but sex, danger and darkness were replaced by humour and lightness. Until, that is, the British film industry took over where 1940s Los Angeles had left us hanging.

Whether in film noir or in British Kitchen Sink drama, the bedroom became a place of anxiety. In *Saturday Night and Sunday Morning* (1960) and *Alfie* (1966) it becomes the scene of seedy flings with married women; the dingy, too-intimate bedrooms of hen-pecked, cuckolded husbands became a place of simultaneous escape and self-loathing.

Nevertheless, bedrooms were allowed back in during the 1960s and 1970s, and the room recovered its image as sex was allowed back into Hollywood: a riot of pink satin and heart-shaped pillows that remained resolutely feminine. If the kitchen has become less of a feminine space as it opens to the rest of the house and becomes a place of the display of macho fixtures, fittings and the performance of preparation, becoming a family and entertaining room, the bedroom curiously persists as a sanctum of the feminine, a place of mirrors and dressing tables, closets, dressing rooms and en suites, a room echoing the rituals of ablution, nakedness, dressing and beautifying. In its association with sex and sleep it is also perhaps the room in which we most truly *dwell*, the place in which we are allowed to dream.

12 CUPBOARDS & WARDROBES

THE WARDROBE AND THE CUPBOARD are the house within the house, their doors open onto an ever more private realm of intimate things. 'Is there any dreamer of words who does not respond to the word *wardrobe*?' asks Gaston Bachelard. 'Every poet of furniture – knows that the inner space of an old wardrobe is deep. A wardrobe's inner space is also *intimate space*, space that is not open to just anybody.'

Rimbaud, in his poem 'The Orphans' New Year's Gift' writes of a wardrobe:

> . . . many a time we dreamed
> Of the mysteries lying dormant between its wooden flanks
> And we thought we heard, deep in the gaping lock
> A distant sound, a vague and joyful murmur.

Literature and film are stuffed with wardrobes as places of refuge, of voyeurism, of intimacy, as symbols of transition to other worlds. C.S. Lewis's *The Lion, the Witch and the Wardrobe* is the most obvious example, in which the wardrobe is not only a gateway to the fairy land of Narnia but a metaphor for the emotional wrench of the childrens' evacuation from London. The voyeuristic possibilities of the wardrobe are explored in countless scenarios, from farce to horror. Most shocking and perhaps most memorable is a scene in David Lynch's *Blue Velvet* in which Kyle Maclachlan's protagonist is forced to hide in a wardrobe watching Isabella Rosselini's character being savagely abused by Dennis Hopper's magnificently unhinged villain and, most unsettlingly, enjoying it. It is equally familiar from farce, the lover hiding from a jealous husband almost a leitmotif for a certain kind of (particularly British) comedy. The idea of a sexualized refuge is reinforced by the phrase 'coming out of the closet', as if the cupboard was a place of sexual confinement, a container of taboo practices.

When writing about his own childhood Freud recalls that his two and a half year old self was anxious that his mother's belly may contain more children and he associates this potential with his mother's wardrobe, the idea there might be more lives lurking in there.

Clothes, the contents of the wardrobe are, of course, intimate items, their tailoring and their physical proximity to the body make them proxies for the corporeal. René Magritte's naturally absurdly titled *En Hommage à Mack Sennett* shows a wardrobe, its door open and a gown suspended within displaying its very real breasts. It is a dream image that reveals something about the fantasy nature of the closet.

Magritte's wardrobe, like Rimbaud's, is a freestanding cupboard. The wardrobe was an expensive piece of furniture which was moved from dwelling to dwelling – so it became a point of consistent reference, a house within a house which always stayed the same no matter what the house on the outside. It was this consistency – alongside the intimacy of its contents and its almost anthropomorphic presence in the bedchamber – which led it to become associated with a kind of private life.

Even the act of locking with a key brings forth undeniable sexual connotations. Arguably, recent trends in furniture design – a combination of the stripping back of detail and a fashion for built-in cupboards – have changed the wardrobe from a talisman to a far less complex extension of the wall, and perhaps this is the reason that designers have begun to re-examine the surreal possibilities of the wardrobe and as a freestanding but decidedly architectural element. Tord Boontje's *Fig Leaf Wardrobe* envisages the cupboard as a kind of Eden, the leaves a suggestive reference, the tree-shaped hanger within a further allusion to paradise and recalls Freud's maternal association. Studio Job's *Robber Baron Cabinet* is a kitsch, gold-leafed fantasy with an unsettling shell-hole through its centre, a decidedly disturbing image of decadent but damaged domesticity. Finally, Studio Wieki Somers' *Cigar Box Wardrobe* takes the eponymous box and attenuates it to create a striking piece of furniture marked by its adherence to the vocabulary of the simple wooden container with its labels and its particular brass hinges, while elsewhere a rash of recent suitcase-style wardrobes seems to emphasize portability deliberately opposed to the contemporary fashion for the built-in.

After many years of being the kind of thing a couple would acquire as part of a wedding gift or on HP with their first house, the wardrobe nearly became defunct, the dressing room and the flush-fitted cupboard conspiring to consign it to the junk shop. But its return in recent design seems to indicate a sentiment and a yearning for the symbolism of the freestanding wardrobe, the compelling idea of a mini-house within a house. Now it appears as a statement, a frank expression of its symbolism and association, not, any more, a box in which to hide clothes (or lovers) away but a sculpture with which to express something of the intimacy of the dream-space of the bedroom. Welcome back wardrobes.

13   Bathrooms

Fʀᴏᴍ ᴛʜᴇ ʙᴀᴛʜ ᴏғ ᴘѕʏᴄʜᴇ to the shower scene in *Psycho* – Lord Leighton to Janet Leigh – the bathroom scene in popular culture has always embodied an exotic eroticism. Leighton's languid Greek goddess, first exhibited in 1889, sheds her last veil to step into the classical bath just as Janet Leigh's character disrobes to cleanse herself of her crime – before she is shredded through a plastic curtain by Norman Bates dressed up as his mother.

Both works open a titillating scene tinged with a hint of danger against the backdrop of the bathroom, but a bathroom of very different types. Leighton depicts the version that Cecil B. DeMille would adopt (the director inserted a bathing scene into every film): the opulently attended bath of columns and marble. Hitchcock employs the functional private anonymity of the white-tiled motel. Psyche looks demurely down at her reflection in the water, Leigh's face in the shower reveals a kind of ecstasy, the pure enjoyment of having sins washed away – although the scene ends with the awful stillness of her eye melded into the water swirling down the plughole.

Between these two archetypes lies the essence of the modern bathroom. Simultaneously the most contemporary and the most antique of rooms, the bathroom only recently became a staple of domestic architecture, yet it is, of course, nothing new. One house in Pompeii features the most extraordinary vaulted, frescoed bathroom whilst two thousand years before that the queen's bathroom in Mari, Mesopotamia featured a pair of sunken baths – one for washing, the other for rinsing. Even earlier (around 1800 BC), at the Palace of King Minos at Knossos in Crete, the architect Daedalus designed an en suite bathroom for the queen. The walls were decorated with friezes and the earthenware bath was very recognisably the same typology as our own fittings.

Despite the Cretan queen's luxurious en suite bedchamber, for most of its early life bathing was a communal rather than a private activity. The Romans famously used the bathhouse as a space of luxury and of socializing, a tradition enthusiastically adopted by the Ottomans who followed them, and the buildings of the two empires, from the awesome vaults of the Baths of Caracalla in Rome to the Cağaloğlu Bath in Istanbul with its star-perforated dome, were secular spaces imbued with the aura of the sacred – bathing was as much ritual as it was practical. Every religion has a form of ritual purification involving water, from the ablutions of Islam to the Mikveh bath of Jewish tradition, from the bathing in the Ganges of the Hindus to the steam baths of Native Americans. There is also a lingering symbolism of renewal and rebirth. To immerse oneself in the warm waters of a bath is to relive the experience of the womb. That feeling of warm forgetting, of a washing away of worries with bathing is a memory.

Medieval palaces and castles may have lacked bathrooms but they may well have had baths – it was a less dirty era than is sometimes imagined. A large wooden barrel placed by the fireside would have served as a bath and it might have been lined with linen to prevent splinters. Curtains might be draped above the bath to create a steam-bath effect and the water might be infused with herbs. Smellies in the bathroom are nothing new; it all adds to the sense of ritual.

The domestic bathroom abandoned since the Romans re-emerged with the introduction of piped water in the nineteenth century. For the centuries in between, the bedchamber and the bathroom were one and the same, a washstand and a chamber pot provided the discreet, mobile furniture of evacuation and ablution – although there were exceptions – the Palace of Versailles famously featuring over a hundred bathrooms. Yet there was nothing particularly private about the act of washing. The wealthy were served, washed and dressed by servants whilst the poor, right up to the twentieth century, bathed in a portable tin or copper bath in the kitchen.

The adoption of the separate bathroom in the mid-to-late nineteenth century privatized the act of ablution, fetishizing its intimacy. The bathroom lock is as new as the flush toilet – which although it was invented in the sixteenth century did not come into widespread use till the mid-nineteenth.

The English were in the vanguard of bathing. Sent to England to study our strange ways in an act of architectural anthropology, German architect and diplomat Hermann Muthesius summed up an attitude of the English bathroom: 'there are disappointments in store for the visitor to England who expects really luxurious bath installations like those demanded by well-to-do home-owners on the continent. Large chambers with domed ceilings, opulent colour schemes . . . a marble bath sunk into the centre of the floor and billowing cushions in the recesses are conspicuous by their absence.' But he goes on to say 'The bathroom is always the simple, plain room dictated by need . . . fundamentally modest and unpretentious. It is alien to the nature of an Englishman of standing to envelop himself in luxury.' Muthesius' conclusion also perfectly summarizes his admiration for the particular architecture of England.

When Muthesius was conducting his research, around the dawn of the twentieth century, the bathroom was fast becoming the technological nerve centre of the house. While other rooms had remained relatively static, fixed around fireplaces, windows and furniture that had barely changed in centuries, the bathroom was an experimental space of modernity. Hot and cold running water piped directly to baths, basins and showers, heated towel rails, extraordinarily complex steam-punk shower cages and flushing water closets (always, in an English home at least, separated from the space for bathing – their combination was an American invention), the architectural language was semi-industrial, copper pipes and nickel-plated brass, taps like the valves of great engines, the white tiles and gleaming porcelain of austere hygiene against which any hint of dirt would show up. Before the aesthetics of modern architecture had developed in the living room they were already embedded in the bathroom.

It was the space of health and efficiency, the room in which architecture would be stripped as naked as the body immersing itself in the waters within. The bathroom was a room with nothing to hide and nowhere to hide it. That aesthetic of raw, naked functionalism, however, was co-opted by an emerging architecture of public health. White tiles, porcelain and exposed pipes became the *de facto* expression of the hospital, of medicalization and, once the hospital became a place of dreary fear rather than the hygienic ray of hope in which it found its genesis, the domestic bathroom became necessarily something else; it became, instead, a vehicle for self-expression.

The contemporary bathroom is a space that is expected to embody contrast and paradox. The language of pampering, of the luxury and decadence so abhorred by Muthesius has returned and taken over – luxurious materials, assorted expensive unguents and scented candles now create a secular shrine of the most functional of spaces and it has become one of the most expensively appointed of rooms. The movies, as ever, have played their role. Whether in the scenes of Elizabeth Taylor's Cleopatra bathing in ass's milk, Marilyn Monroe's toe stuck in the faucet in *Seven Year Itch* or Victoria Abril's innovative use of a wind-up toy in Almodovar's *Tie Me Up! Tie Me Down!*, movies, TV and ads have attempted to portray the bathroom as a realm of sensuality and female luxury. It is usually women shown luxuriating in baths and it is similarly often associated with sex.

We could say that the bathroom is one of the few spaces to have succumbed to a recognition of the importance of symbolism. The gleaming, super-expensive taps, the huge rainwater shower-heads and mirror-polished controls are all fittings that recognize the act of purification as symbolic ritual. Whether they are swan-shaped taps or minimalist spouts these things are moments of memory.

At the same time, the combination of WC and bath, a very symbolic cocktail, reminds us of the most basic of urges, Freud's anal fixation. The extraordinary proliferation of bathrooms throughout the house has become a kind of architectural metastasis with en suites and cloakrooms sprouting up and swallowing space as they swallow our waste. These conflicting ideas of purification, evacuation, opulence, minimalism and the need for a subtly sexualized shrine to self-administered luxury and the retreat to the sanctuary of the bath waters make for one of the most symbolically loaded of modern rooms. It is a heavy burden for the bathroom to carry but perhaps it is precisely this constantly shifting kaleidoscope of meaning and fashion that makes the bathroom as brutally honest a reflection of our domestic concerns as the bathroom mirror does of our bodies.

14 IRONMONGERY & HARDWARE

FINNISH ARCHITECT JUHANI PALLASMAA calls the door handle 'the handshake of a building'. Architecture might be the most physical of the arts but it is also, as Palasmaa has pointed out in his beautiful book *The Eyes of the Skin* (2005), one in which the sense of vision is hugely privileged over all the others. Architects talk incessantly about light and space, about shadow, solid and void, but rarely about texture and weight, about how something feels in the hand or what effects a surface can exert on the body. Ironmongery presents us with one of the few moments when we are forced to physically and haptically engage with the building, so perhaps it's surprising that most dwellings by default feature standard, mass-manufactured and shoddily-designed products that tell us little or nothing about the way we use a building, about the rituals or meanings of passing from one space to another or about the way we use them. Of course, I've got form in this area, I co-founded a hardware manufacturer (izé) in 2001 and have been thinking about ironmongery ever since, even when I didn't really want to. But this involvement in the design and manufacture of all kinds of ironmongery has given me an insight into the possibilities inherent in a seemingly mundane moment in architecture. Even the word 'ironmongery' in English ('hardware' in the US) is so generic, so quotidian that it seems to offer little inspiration. Perhaps precisely because it has been ignored for so long, it seems like the most fruitful of territories for symbol, meaning and for the potential of physically interacting with the material of the house.

The totem of the front door and the place we have to start is the knocker, a mechanism which both announces arrival and allows the visitor to engage with the building through touch. One of the oldest, most familiar motifs is that of the hand, perhaps bearing a ball, which acts to knock against a backplate. Perhaps Palasmaa is wrong and it is the knocker which first shakes our hand. The knocker might also be an animal's head, but is just as likely to be some kind of abstract composition based upon ill-suited off-the-shelf classical motifs, an undersized trophy resembling a cremation urn or a spindly volute. This means that the most visceral and ritual of actions tends to be mediated through a flimsy, poorly conceived amalgam of half-remembered shapes. In fact, all these forms have a deep history that chimes with the knocker's symbolic role. It's impossible not to think of Dickens' *A Christmas Carol* and Jacob Marley's face appearing to Scrooge on a dark night, an image which sends a chill down the spine but which also brings to mind the association of the knocker with a living thing – or at least the ghost of memory of a living thing.

The lion's head is amongst the most familiar motifs, or perhaps a fox or a horseshoe. Perhaps it might be a monster's head with a ring in its mouth, a fiery demon (which was a popular choice for church doors). Each of these forms embodies a memory of a time when spirits were thought to dwell by doors, around thresholds and openings. These might be evil or friendly spirits, the ghosts of deceased relatives or the devil himself. When someone sneezes and someone's pipes up with a 'bless you', we are re-enacting a blessing to ensure the devil could not enter through a nose – as the moments after a sneeze were seen as a vulnerable opening in which the body was laid bare to evil. The opening of a door is a similar moment in which we leave ourselves open. The knocker provides a semblance of symbolic protection.

If it is your own home you are likely to use a key to enter. There is an obvious sexual connotation in the action, just as there is in the penetration of the door into the womb-like house (indeed also in the idea of the letterbox), yet, once again this most symbolic of acts is rarely celebrated in the architecture in what seems a terrible lost opportunity. A brief wander through the Victoria & Albert Museum's metalwork galleries reveals an almost unimaginable array of exquisitely sculpted and wrought keys. Throughout the Middle Ages and the Renaissance these elaborate keys were ritual fetishes which spoke of the grandeur of the contents, teasing and delighting. Technology is now moving towards biometric locks, machines which range from thumbprint, voice and iris recognition. This may be more to justify the expense of top-end developments but the intimate relationship of door and lock with the body does seem to resurrect these ancient associations.

Front doors might feature a central doorknob, but these are partly aesthetic and more for closing the door behind you than for opening it from the outside (front doors open inwards in a gesture of welcome). Once inside though, the doors rely on very functional handles. Your progress through the house is defined by a series of grips and twists which, apart from the handrail on the stairs and perhaps a light switch, are likely to be the only moments you get to engage with the materiality of the interior. The oldest door-opening device was a simple metal ring, a pull, a device that has achieved near universality. A slightly more sophisticated mechanism which combined lock and handle in one was the thumb-latch, a piece of hardware still popular in the US, far less so in Europe where doorknobs and later levers became ubiquitous after the Renaissance. The basic wooden knob was turned from a solid chunk of timber and the manner of its making, the spinning, carving motion prefigures the way it works, the twisting, rotating motion of opening.

The particular grip you need to engage with a doorknob forces on you a very intimate relationship with the material. With wood, each user leaves their trace on the timber (sweat, oil, dirt), older examples being polished to a dark sheen through the wear of the traces from thousands of hands. From around the end of the Renaissance knobs were commonly made of metal, the most elaborate example from French palaces equalling the repoussé work of the great goldsmiths, extraordinarily elaborate decorative forms which leave the faint imprints of scrolls and cherub's heads upon your palm, stamping the architecture briefly onto the most sensitive of flesh. At first the knobs were placed on rim-locks (locks fitted on to one side of the door), in which the locks were as decorated as the handles then, by the nineteenth century, the lock mechanism became discreetly buried in the thickness of the door and only the handles remained exposed. Around the same time the lever handle, which had been around for centuries, began to become popular, particularly in Europe. The Modernists in particular delighted in the lever's tool-like functionalism. Walter Gropius's 1923 design became perhaps the most ubiquitous and successful product to emerge from the Bauhaus (and one of the very few products to have made money for the persistently beleaguered art school), a deceptively simple object which managed to reconcile the Platonic perfection of the square and the circle in the cylindrical grip and the square neck and backplate. In its abstract forms we can see the radical art of Malevich and the Suprematists. It remains one of the most popular and enduring Modernist products.

The early Modernist period saw an explosion in handle design, from the elegant stripped-back rationalism of Wilhelm Wagenfeld's 1926 design in which a circle is taken apart, its missing quarter suggesting the downward rotation of the lever, to the crystalline, jagged forms of Expressionism and their populist offspring: the stepped, layered, Aztec-influenced designs of Art Deco which once appeared in every suburban home of the inter-war building boom yet which have almost entirely disappeared from our interiors – doors have proved particularly susceptible to the vagaries of fashion.

But it was a philosopher who arguably, and extraordinarily, exerted the greatest impact on the modern handle. Having studied engineering, Ludwig Wittgenstein, who was designing his sister's house in Vienna (1926–7), became transfixed by the possibilities of engineering material and designed a handle from simple bent metal tube. One side featured the now ubiquitous design, the steel handle you can see in every office block and every institutional building across the developed world. The other side, however, featured a double curve, a more complex bend. Handles had always been (and still nearly always are) symmetrical, the same on both sides of the door. Wittgenstein's design implied a hierarchy, an acknowledgement of the difference between spaces, between reception room and hall, representational space and servant space. I had always thought that it was this desire to bring hierarchy to handle design, to begin to acknowledge something of the different nature of the space on one side as opposed to the other which had led

Wittgenstein to this idea. In fact, when I visited the house, I realized that he'd done it to avoid clashing with a steel mullion on a pair of French windows. Necessity, it seems, really is the mother of invention.

Ultimately though it was his simple tube that was adopted to become the most familiar handle in the world, a dumb bent stainless steel pipe which has arguably nearly killed invention and interpretation in hardware. It took Wittgenstein over a year to design (he spent the next two designing a radiator), but it is one that has added little richness to our lives. The ubiquitous bent tube has reduced the most symbolic of architectural acts to a mechanical function.

Recent years have seen a return to favour for doorknobs, perhaps a reaction against the ubiquity and institutional aesthetic of stainless steel levers. Cast bronze and brass knobs are reappearing on domestic doors. They become a kind of punctuation mark, either a full stop or a comma, symbols at the end of a sequence that entice you to carry on a little further.

15

DOORS

ORE THAN ANY OTHER ARCHITECTURAL ELEMENT, the door has saturated our language as a metaphor so fully that we barely even notice it. We might talk about being at death's door, knocking on heaven's door or about the girl next door. We might read about the doors of perception, hear about a door-to-door salesman getting a foot in the door. You might beat a path to someone's door or leave your attitude or check your weapons at the door. You might keep the wolf from the door or shut the stable door after the horse has bolted. The list appears almost endless and the reason is clear, the door is the most obvious expression of transition from one realm to another, a slightly magical mechanism that makes a solid wall permeable.

The idea of the door as opening into another, unknown realm is among the most recurrent tropes in fairy tales and literature, in film and fable. There is something faintly sinister about a locked door, but also something irresistibly tempting. In the tale of Bluebeard's Castle, popularized by Charles Perrault and subsequently reinforced by Béla Bartók, the heroine is told not to open the locked door in the castle. Of course she can't resist and slips the key in, opening the door to find the still bloody bodies of her husband's former wives. She shuts and locks the door in horror but finds that the blood won't wash off the key or the door, no matter how hard she scrubs. The sexual symbolism is powerfully present. Marina Warner suggests that the bloodied bodies represent the shocking arrival of menstruation. In fact the door appears in many myths and tales as a portal for girls between childhood and adulthood, from Lewis Carroll's *Alice's Adventures in Wonderland* to Guillermo del Toro's *Pan's Labyrinth*, small doors appear in stories which echo the archetypal tales of temptation from Adam and Eve to Pandora's Box, stories in which young girls are unable to resist the temptation to open doors which might take them to dangerous places. When Judy Garland's Dorothy opens her door after her house is picked up by a tornado in *The Wizard of Oz*, cinema comes up with one of its greatest ever sleights of hand. The world she opens the door on to is in full garish Technicolor, while the world she left behind in Kansas was in dreary black and white. She is awakening.

Jung is extremely clear about the sexual nature of doors, about their symbolism of penetration. And something of this sense of danger and sexuality has passed down to us from superstition. Doors were considered active places in old houses, places where the spirits of the house might reside and where evil spirits may enter. If the front door was characterized by sun symbolism, the back door related to the night, to darkness. If someone died in a house, the body might not be taken out through the front door but through the back (or even through a door specially made in the wall and then bricked up again – so as to avoid the ghost of the departed re-entering the house). A horseshoe might be hung above the back door (its arms always pointing upward to prevent the luck from running out), the symbol of the crescent moon but also perhaps echoing the shape of a vessel or container of good luck, a glass of wine. It is no coincidence that we bring bottles of wine as housewarming gifts, to bless the house. Those bottles also recall one of the strangest, most unsettling manifestations of belief in witchcraft, once a common feature in houses: witch bottles. These were small glass or terracotta flasks built into walls, often above doors (or in fireplaces) and prepared by witches for homeowners fearful of spells being cast against them. They would contain a few strands of hair, perhaps nail clippings and even urine and menstrual blood, alongside needles and herbs. The belief was that the charms and spells would be caught up in the bottle, misdirected by the contents and torn apart on the pins and needles.

The doors themselves might also contain deep seams of symbolism. Panelled doors might be split into four sections relating to the four cardinal points, so that the door becomes a map of the known world, a plan inscribed in timber with a crucifix at its centre. Or they might feature six panels, a vertical tripartite division representing the body, legs, torso and head. I hardly need to go into detail about the knob.

Elsewhere, the elements of the door that make it secure might be exaggerated, made bold in a symbolic attempt to convince physical or spiritual intruders of their strength. Locks, which are now routed into the depth of the door, were once bolted to one side, heavy iron boxes with rich decoration. The more elaborate they were, the more obviously difficult they would be to open. Strap hinges were made into decorative elements, far larger and more elaborate than function alone demanded. Small openings at eye height might be protected with ostentatious iron grilles and magical motifs, hearts and crosses might be carved into timber door leaves. The most visible surviving symbolic tradition can be seen in Orthodox Jewish households, where a Mezuzah might be fixed to the right post of every doorframe (except the bathroom). This is a small vessel, often highly decorated, containing a handwritten verse from the Torah on a parchment scroll. There were conflicting prescriptions and traditions about how these should be affixed to the frame – either pointing up or pointing in toward the room to be entered – as a result of which most are fixed at a slight slant to hedge the bets.

The door has also become one of the most familiar devices in literature and film, a portent of an event to come. 'When in doubt,' said Raymond Chandler, 'have a man come in through the door with a gun in his hand.' Perhaps the similarity of the action of opening a door to the turning of a page has made it an irresistible motif but it is just as common in film where a door forms such a natural transition from one scene or mood to the next. Chandler wrote the screenplay of Billy Wilder's *Double Indemnity*, a film crowded with doors as representations of the permeable boundaries between darkness and light, good and evil, truth and lies. In one of the most famous scenes in the film, Fred McMurray's Walter Neff uses his apartment door to hide his devious lover (Barbara Stanwyck's Phyllis Dietrichson) from his boss Edward G. Robinson. Stanwyck is in the shade cast by the door, in the dark just like a film noir femme fatale should be. But perhaps the most extraordinary door scene occurs in Hitchcock's *Spellbound* (1945) in which Ingrid Bergman closes her eyes to get kissed by Gregory Peck (the mysterious head of an insane asylum) and a series of doors begins to open. It is as subtle as a train going through a tunnel yet it presents an unforgettable image, the door as symbol of the sexual ecstasy Hollywood cinema was so famously banned from showing. Salvador Dalí had been the visual and dream-scene consultant on the film.

In Francis Ford Coppola's *The Godfather* it is the final scene of the door closing which sticks in the memory. Al Pacino's Michael

Corleone has been anointed the new Godfather, succeeding his father and the family supplicates to him, kissing his hand as the door is closed, excluding Michael's wife, Kaye (Diane Keaton). She is shut out of the family in a single, shockingly brutal gesture, which seems nothing more than the simple closing of a door.

Elsewhere in Spike Jonze's *Being John Malkovich*, a door is discovered in a dead-end office (itself stuck between two floors so it is only half normal height), which leads into the eponymous actor's mind. It is the most extraordinary and literal device, with no metaphor or symbol showing, just straight into the head. When Malkovich himself barges in, he finds a sinister world populated entirely by Malkoviches, simulacra of himself.

There is nothing new in the idea of a door as a symbol of the mind. Darren Aronofsky's profoundly unsettling film *Pi*, about an increasingly unhinged and disturbed mathematical genius, uses the blinding white light from behind a door as a symbol perhaps of clarity, perhaps of death, perhaps of heaven, but certainly a cipher for an imploding mind. It is also obviously a symbol of the passing from one state to another, life to death, profane to sacred, ephemeral to eternal and so on. In this way the door, which is partly open, represents temptation, the irresistible urge to explore. When is a door not a door? When it's ajar. I'd guess that's the oldest, corniest Christmas cracker joke there is. But it actually tells us something interesting about the condition of the door. A door that is open is one thing, a door that is shut is another, but a door that is partly open offers a glimpse of something beyond. It hints perhaps at the state between consciousness and dreaming but also at the idea of voyeurism, the glimpse of something forbidden, a snatch of overheard conversation or a momentary eyeful of forbidden fruit. The beginnings of the movies themselves lie in this idea of a gaze into the forbidden. The fairground 'What the Butler Saw' machines, cranked by hand and slowly revealing an undressing girl, are framed as a view through a door or perhaps a keyhole. Pornography always manages to make new media work for it.

Because the door is such a powerful framing device, the exact way it opens is never a random decision. Instead the way a door is hung defines the moment of transition from one space to another and the critical first impression of a new space. In that scene in *Double Indemnity* where Barbara Stanwyck hides behind the door, the production designer needed to hang the doors the wrong way round, opening out into the corridor instead of opening into the apartment which is how they always work (otherwise people walking down the corridor would be liable to get smacked in the face Laurel and Hardy style by opening doors). The director figured no one would notice – and he was almost certainly right. Yet the action of pushing a door open and revealing the space beyond is pivotal to our sense of propriety in inhabiting and moving through space – it is a gesture of revealing but also of opening up – the inwards motion of the door indicating a welcome. In grand continental houses and apartments, doors would generally be placed as centrally as possible in the wall of a room so that from within the wall would appear symmetrical and the furniture within it could be arranged as evenly as possible. The ultimate result of this desire for symmetry and grandeur is the suite of enfilade rooms. These are interconnecting spaces which open into each other (usually via double doors) to create a grand vista through a series of rooms which flow into one another in a long line – the grandeur emphasized by the perspective. This is an architecture of appearances, one inspired by palaces and royal egos. Its influence can be seen in smaller domestic settings where the two ground floor or first floor reception rooms might often feature a pair of tall double doors allowing them to be connected for a big social event. The effect is usually spoilt by the typical British plan featuring a rear extension which will ensure the back window of the two spaces will not be aligned with the front, ruining the illusion of a properly planned palatial progression.

British houses generally developed a different etiquette, one not based on a desire for enfilade rooms but rather one predicated on the idea of privacy and discretion. Hermann Muthesius, in *The English House*, commented on how doors in English houses would be placed at one end of a wall and would open away from the corner thus momentarily shielding the view of the room from the new entrant, giving those already in the room a moment to compose themselves before receiving the new guest. This arrangement also, as Muthesius points out, leaves more room on the walls of even modest sized homes for imposing pieces of furniture and for art.

The etymology of the word 'door' highlights its centrality to language and its importance as a component of the dwelling. It comes to us from the Sanskrit *dvarah*, via the Old English *duru* and, intriguingly, its Sanskrit and ancient uses tend to be in the plural which has led to some speculation that the doors of our ancestors might have been double. If we think of something as modest as the flaps of a tent or as imposing the doors of temple or cathedral, it is indeed the symmetry of the double door we see, an elemental idea which allows doors to be ritually thrown open in a clear gesture of welcome and invitation. The doors are the first and most symbolic element of architecture, they convey the meaning of privacy and security, their form crystallizes the position and meaning of the threshold.

16 WINDOWS

IT MAY BE A CLICHÉ, but if the eyes are the windows to the soul, that would make the windows the eyes of a house. And etymology suggests that is exactly what they are. Our word derives from the Norse *vindauga* from *vind* ('wind') and *auga* ('eye'). The original wind-eye was the oculus (also Latin for 'eye', from the same Sanskrit root), the hole in the middle of a roof that allowed smoke from the fire to escape. Windows are the apertures through which we communicate with the outside world, but they work both ways. They allow light in but allow us to look out and, as anyone who has travelled on an urban train or double-decker bus on a winter night (or, as a child, peered up close in through the windows of a doll's house) knows, they draw outsiders inexorably in. It is nearly impossible to prevent your gaze from wandering into the private lives of others made suddenly visible.

When I first stayed in a New York apartment I found myself gazing, mesmerized, at the man-made cliff punctuated by an infinite array of illuminated scenes from lives being played out in front of me. There were couples sitting, eating in silence, there were others arguing, watching TV, doing their hair or make up, adjusting their ties. Each window becomes a device to frame a life, a screen – something Hitchcock was powerfully aware of when he made *Rear Window*, in which wheelchair-bound James

Stewart cannot resist being drawn into the lives of those opposite and extrapolating narratives.

The window as the frame for the voyeur is also one of the most consistent motifs in art. In Edward Hopper's night-time scenes it provides glimpses into isolated, atomized modern lives in which lonely figures are illuminated by the sterile glare of naked bulbs. In *Room in New York* (1932), a woman listlessly pokes a finger at a piano keyboard while her husband reads the paper. They are together, but apart.

Magritte parallels the view through the window with that on the canvas, the painting replacing the window pane, whilst Dalí depicts his wife Gala looking yearningly at the sea beyond (beautifully illustrating Freud's notion of the window as a pseudo-sexual opening in the body of the house). It can be hard to see any abstract planes, from Mark Rothko's sunset planes to Dan Flavin's fluorescent frames, as anything other than pure, minimal representations of the window.

The window is, in its way, the basic unit of architecture. Every house has windows and it is the form of the openings, the patterns they make on the façade, the rhythms they establish in the city which forms the particular urban language just as they become the outward expression of the humblest cottage. The window began as a simple opening with no membrane, perhaps only a shutter. These were not windows for looking out but for bringing what was outside – light and air – in. Slowly they evolved into bigger openings, initially with leaded lights which allowed light in but did not allow significant views out. It was only in the seventeenth century that the technology emerged to make bigger sheets of glass and this represented a radical change. Suddenly the window became a device which framed a view of the world outside. What this view achieves is the effect of removing the viewer from the context and imposing an order on the world outside, it is easily comparable to a film screen, which also appears as a window onto another world. This new type of window for looking as well as for lighting brings with it a very definite separation between the world and the interior.

The membrane itself, the glass, is also an interface with the elements. The panes rattle in the wind, the water taps against it in the rain and forms droplets which trickle down to distort the view into a beaded veil. Windows afford a view but they also subtly distort it, frame it and change it. The gaze framed through a window is something very different to the panoramic view outside.

The Brothers Grimm were the most assiduous of collectors of folklore and myth, their fairy tales precursors to Jung and his archetypes. Their fairy tale 'Snow White' begins like this:

> Once upon a time in the middle of winter, when the
> flakes of snow were falling like feathers from the sky,
> a queen sat at a window sewing, and the frame of the
> window was made of black ebony. And whilst she was
> sewing and looking out of the window at the snow, she
> pricked her finger with the needle, and three drops of
> blood fell upon the snow. And the red looked pretty
> upon the white snow, and she thought to herself,
> would that I had a child as white as snow, as red as
> blood, and as black as the wood of the window-frame.

That child, of course, became Snow White. Disney's film too begins with a window, the elaborate grated window of a castle, but this time of the wicked witch and as the film zooms in through the window the queen approaches her mirror to ask 'Magic Mirror on the wall, who is the fairest one of all.' The answer, as we know, is Snow White. The correspondence made here, between window and mirror is intriguing, both reflecting and predicting, the blood on the snow, the monstrous magic mirror.

The Virgin Mary is also associated with the window and representations, most notably in Renaissance scenes, are almost guaranteed to depict a window nearby, particularly in scenes of the Annunciation. The symbolic implication is that the Virgin is so pure that the light from heaven shines right through her – effectively impregnating her, so that the window stands for the hymen. Arguably the most beautiful depictions of interiors in art history depict this theme. Fra Filippo Lippi's version (c.1450) in Rome's Galleria Doria-Pamphili is the most literal, the hands of God releasing the dove representing the Holy Spirit which subsequently flies in through the window and from which radiates the heavenly light pointing towards her womb. But others include Botticelli's sublime work of 1489 (in which the window is part door/part frame for a landscape) and Bellini's Annunciation, in which Gabriel kneels outside an arcade (in a city street very much like a stage set) looking in. Each of these paintings presents the scene as a theatrical set piece with the architecture as central as the characters and each has their corresponding symbol in the building.

These Renaissance windows were leaded or shuttered, occasionally even featuring stained glass roundels depicting the Virgin herself (as in Petrus Christus' Annunciation of 1452, set in a gothic church). But as technology improved and panes of glass could be made flatter, bigger and better, the types of windows changed too.

Among the many types of windows, the sash has been historically most associated with Holland, Britain (and its former colonies) and the USA, and the casement with Europe and the rest of the world. These two mechanisms offer very different meanings. The casement is pulled or thrown open, like a door, in a gesture of allowing the outside in but also of theatrically opening the house to the world. The sash is far more reserved. It can be opened at the top only, to let in a gentle breeze above head level, but never thrown open completely. Something odd happens as glass becomes more perfect. If we look at the paintings of Edward Hopper we see that the glass has disappeared entirely and returned to the open state of the Renaissance Italian Annunciations of the balmy Tuscan summer. Hopper's lonely, alienated individuals all seem to be framed through a window – in which case we get voyeuristic glimpses of lives we know nothing about, or are looking through windows staring at the blank streets outside. These sashes appear very much like frames, or perhaps like film screens, openings onto worlds which seem to suggest a lack of connection between the individual and the city outside. Even the title of Hopper's *Morning in a City* suggests the anonymity of the streets, its naked protagonist lost and staring out at something that seems simultaneously familiar and alien. In *Morning Sun*, the protagonist's slip is short, her legs drawn up, the light floods in. There is no angel Gabriel yet the inference is of those scenes of the Virgin penetrated by light. The same could be said of *Night Windows* where the room is viewed from an impossible angle outside and above, the girl bending over her backside to the window, the sash a perfect frame to an imperfectly seen scene.

The massive changes in construction technology during the nineteenth century dramatically shifted the boundaries of the window. What had been an opening in a solid wall became an almost limitless possibility as the load-bearing function of the building was shifted to an iron or steel frame. Windows could become as big as the wall itself, they could become the wall. Whilst early Modernist architects assumed this transparency would open up our lives, freeing us of the dark corners and hidden nooks, it actually led to something else. A glazed wall is a very different proposition to a window, the framing is removed, the viewer is placed back into the world outside but becomes equally visible to the outside. It turned out we rather liked those hidden corners and, except for a few experiments in tower blocks and self-conscious villas, our modern windows are very recognisably those of four centuries ago, in fact, in most contemporary housing, considerably worse.

The existential blankness of these windows is exacerbated by their lack of grounding, they are frameless frames. Just as contemporary art has dispensed with the decorated frame, most architects have abandoned the idea of a framing device. The surround does not have to be elaborate but it is critical. The aedicule in which a classical window sat was a miniature building with base, columns and pediment, privileging the importance of the opening as a moment of transition between worlds. Whether it is the hewn stone of a portico around the window of a Renaissance Palace or the simple rubbed brick arch and plain painted sill around a the openings of a Georgian terrace, the window cannot exist in isolation, it needs situating in the wall. The reveal (the set back from the façade), the sill, the sub-divisions of glazing, the ironmongery, shutters, frame, architraves, the reflections in the glass, we read each of these elements in the same way as we look into one another's eyes when we talk. The windows, more than any other feature, speak to us from outside and in.

17 FACADES & FACES

GROWING OUT OF THE LANDSCAPE in the Renaissance gardens at Bomarzo, near Rome, are a number of strange creatures. Carved out of the rocks, they take the form of monsters' heads, their screaming maws prickled with teeth, their dark throats inviting us to take a look into a fissure in the landscape. They draw you in, almost mesmerically. The word 'monster' derives from the same roots as the word 'demonstrate' and these demonic heads show us something of the nature of what's behind and of ourselves: a face from a different, dream-like world.

That is not to say the façade (a word which derives from the Latin *facies*, 'face') is always monstrous; it can be welcoming as well as a warning. But it is, either way, very closely related to humanity and always a little bit alive.

Get a small child to draw a house and you'll almost certainly see the face emerge. It's clearly there in the little house in the woods that is the stock set of the northern European fairy tales. And we reference it when we say someone is putting on a 'façade'.

The cottage provides our clearest archetype. The thatched roof approximates to hair, the windows to eyes, the door to a mouth. This is a house that could protect you – but also eat you up.

The window (or wind-eye) is the element that most closely resembles its function in the face; it is the opening for seeing. If eyes are the windows to the soul, then windows are the eyes by which a house and its inhabitants are judged and through which the world is perceived. We have a tendency to inscribe ourselves upon the things that are most important to us. The house presents our image of ourselves to the world, so it inevitably begins to take on anthropomorphic characteristics, even if these have been obscured by centuries of refinement and development.

The Modern movement, with its white walls and dull expanses of glass, has dimmed the relationship between body and dwelling; rather than becoming an expression of our character, the modern house becomes a screen through which to display a lifestyle. Yet the early Modernists, in all their extraordinary formal range, were well aware of the power of the human metaphor. Even the most alienated of existentialists, Jean-Paul Sartre, could write in *Being and Nothingness* during the trauma of the war: 'My body is everywhere: the bomb which destroys my house also destroys my body insofar as the house was already an indication of my body.'

The monsters of Bomarzo demonstrate a certain horror at the identification with the house; an entering into another realm of fantasy and fear. The 'hellmouths' that appear in the fearsome paintings of Hieronymus Bosch and Pieter Brueghel envisage the entrance to the darkness of the nether worlds as monstrous, teeth-baring heads and were based on theatrical props of the same era, which produced Bomarzo. In an early slapstick short film *The Haunted House* by Segundo de Chomon (1908), we get a glimpse of the little tumbledown cottage as a crazed faced, its pupils spinning and the chimney transforming into a top hat worn at a jaunty angle.

The same feeling of the uncanny hits us viscerally when we see works that interpret the anthropomorphism of the façade too literally. In Federico Zuccari's sixteenth-century Palazzo Zuccari in Rome, the doors and windows turn into screaming, angry visages; Antoni Gaudí's blocks morph into balcony-front masks and sinister anthropomorphic chimney pots in *fin-de-siècle* Barcelona; Hungarian architect Imre Makovecz created houses with faces as a gesture of rebellion against the facelessness of a bureaucratic communist regime. He also imagined an archetypal house, an image of how a house-being might appear to those who originally conceived it as a living thing, a protective, sentient being animated by spirits. Even in the works of the severe Modernist Adolf Loos, faces clearly emerge as the house begins to take on the characteristics of its client.

When the Post Modernist architects questioned the banality of the Modernist façade, they countered facelessness with, er… facefulness. A rash of jokey houses from the 1960s onwards were inspired by the rediscovery of commercial kitsch in Las Vegas in Robert Venturi, Denise Scott Brown and Stephen Izenour's *Learning from Las Vegas* (1972). The authors wrote of the joys of buildings that were pure signs, facades designed to be noticed from the freeway whilst travelling at speed. These might be a giant hot dog or a duck, a smoking cowboy or a clown's face. Architects leapt at the opportunity to create playful facades with real character.

Of course, this is not the only reading of the façade, merely the most literal and, hopefully, poetic. For most of architectural history, the façade has been a device for representing decorum, in the rhythm of its openings or the richness of its materials and mouldings. The English Georgian terrace can seem a world away from the monstrous maws of mannerism. Yet even in the most rational of houses, the human metaphor can be close by. In his incomparable 1958 film *Mon Oncle*, Jacques Tati parodied the Modernist villa with a ridiculous face that appears as the *bourgeois* inhabitants peer out from, moving in synchrony, porthole eyes becoming like roving pupils.

What is most enticing about the idea of the face of a house is that it allows us to see the house behind it as the mind. And it allows us not just to read the rooms but to psychoanalyse them. For Sigmund Freud, a dream of a house was about the body; it symbolizes ourselves not only to others but also inside our own heads.

18 BAY WINDOWS & BALCONIES

THE BAY WINDOW SEEMS a wonderfully English invention. It is a kind of balcony for the northern climate, an intimately scaled yet bright enclave, which is both inside and outside. The bay breaks through the wall, it encroaches on the public realm but is, of course, entirely within the building. Yet surprisingly, the roots of the bay lie not under the cool grey skies of northern Europe but in the narrow, shaded alleys of the Middle East. The Mashrabiya in Arab houses is a protruding bay contained within a shell of delicate perforated, latticework screens. It is, in complete contrast to its Anglo Saxon derivative, an architectural device for keeping cool. Its name may derive from either of two sources. One of these is a word for a shelf that was placed in the window, upon which earthenware pots were put in order for the liquids in them to be kept cool by the cherished breeze as the water evaporated through the pores in the pot. The other possible origin is the verb *Ashrafa*, to observe. The Mashrabiya allowed a view of the street – of the public realm – without being observed, which was particularly important for the womenfolk: the Mashrabiya as architectural niqab. The intricate geometric patterns, at their best astonishingly beautiful, were often the only decorative element on the austere façades of these fiercely private dwellings.

The bay emerged in Britain in the wonderfully inventive houses of the Tudor era, when their delicate tracery and leaded glass evoked the latticework of the Mashrabiya. But they disappeared again in the classicizing centuries and the symmetrically flat façades that followed. They re-emerged, however, first in the delicately convex windows of the Regency era, the dandified frills of a Beau Brummell bow. But it was the Victorians who resurrected them into an archetypal British domestic motif. Victorian architects and developers revelled in sculptural form and projections that pointedly echoed the layout of the interiors.

The protruding bay window allowed designers to have it both ways. It allowed them a device for denoting the principle rooms and arrangements from the outside (a way of exposing the grandeur and distribution of principle rooms to the outside world) as well as demarcating them from the inside by pushing their envelope beyond the walls of the containing house. But as well as being this proto-functionalist device for expressing how the building worked, it also allowed the builders of quotidian terraces to add a dash of sculptural flair to their structures. The bay became the architectural equivalent of a brooch.

As a pivotal part of the emerging architectural language of English Free Style (the eclectic, all-embracing tolerant style of the 1900 era), the bay also became critically important in the building of the big mansion blocks of the Edwardian era, giving them modelling and relief and hugely enhancing the light inside. But it was also a principle motif of the Arts and Crafts houses (where it was partnered by its cosier, darker equivalent, the inglenook) and it is perhaps during this intensely nostalgic but strangely modern burst of activity around the end of the nineteenth century that the bay window became, arguably, the

110

defining element of the British house. From the Tudor solidity of W.R. Lethaby's Avon Tyrrell House in Hampshire (1891) and the enormous double-height bay of Edwin Lutyens' Deanery Garden in Berkshire (1899) to the exquisite delicacy of Charles Rennie Mackintosh's Hill House, Helensburgh (1903), this brief flowering saw the bay window emerge as a focus of domestic design. From these luxurious, sentimentally nostalgic houses for wealthy industrialists, the bay spread to become the element which added animation to endless rows of terraces and ribbons of suburban semis, an element that could be cheaply and endlessly played with to create a plethora of little architectural expressions on an endless wall of blank façades.

The balcony is the rest of the world's answer to the bay. They haven't got our weather. If the Mashrabiyah and the bay allow residents to blur the boundaries between the interior and the exterior without exposing themselves to the public glare or the weather, the balcony is its theatrical, extrovert urban cousin. Throwing the doors to the balcony wide is a gesture of opening the dwelling up to the city – projecting. That the balcony is a familiar element from both stage and auditorium (where it becomes a box with its multiple connotations of the public display of wealth and appearance, voyeurism and a certain thrill of intimate privacy within a crowd) is no coincidence, it is perhaps the most dramatic of all architectural devices. They allow monarchs, dictators and popes to wave to the masses while also encouraging old ladies to lean on the railings and watch the everyday drama of the street below. The balcony facilitates a level of control over the street or piazza below. It allows the humblest citizen a commanding position above the city. It is the point at which the collective bargaining power of the apartment block most visibly supersedes the detachment of the house. The

111

scale, height and mass of the apartment house is both alleviated by the balcony's mediation between the internal private and the external public realm, but also it imposes itself on the city through that sense of ownership, of the bird's-eye view. But curiously, even though it is a place of power and position, the balcony is also just as capable of becoming a liminal, forgotten space within the city, a kind of aerial garden shed. Quite often it becomes a place for storing things that belong to an outdoors of which an apartment-dweller is deprived. Old plastic chairs and barbecues, bicycles, toy pedal cars, watering cans, plant stands and plant pots, the detritus of a garden which was never there. The lack of storage that seems an inevitable aspect of apartment life paralyses the balcony, transforming the relationship between this small space and the outside from one of overlooking to one of things that have been overlooked. Quite often, particularly in southern and eastern Europe (where shortage of space tends to be most intense), the balcony begins to become a bay as it is first roofed over, then walled up, perhaps with basic glazing. In this stage it can transform into either (if you're lucky) a conservatory or (if you're not) a slum. It becomes the First World equivalent of the informal dwelling, a lean-to shack self-built to solve spatial shortage. This isn't by any means always a bad thing for the architecture – quite often the grimmest of façades are transformed into lively patchworks of inventive adaptation.

For Freud, of course, the balcony was the symbol of the breast, the feminizing projection of the dwelling. Think only of Juliet's plaintive scene and it becomes clear. But, with its decorative iron railings, possibly window boxes, and its projection into the liminal zone between inside and out, it also brings with it the promise of a threshold between artifice and nature. Antoni

Gaudí's surreal balcony fronts at the Casa Mila in Barcelona (1906) appear as seaweed tumbling down the façade (although at the Casa Batlló they become sinister carnival masks).

The Modernists similarly perceived the balcony as an interface between man and nature. The sun and fresh air obsessed architects of the 1920s rather charmingly saw the house as an extension of the balcony or the terrace rather than vice versa. Preoccupied with the blurring of the interior and exterior, through picture and ribbon windows, roof terraces or balconies, these architects purged the house of its traditional elements, of cosiness and intimacy, but the balcony survived, expressed not as the ornate protuberance of the Beaux Arts city but as a nautical quirk. In his proselytizing books Le Corbusier placed photos of ocean liners beside his crisp new villas, the balcony and the terrace became an observation deck on a journey to a new architecture.

19 SHEDS, HUTS & TREEHOUSES

T HE PRIMITIVE HUT is one of the key archetypes in architecture. Every age rediscovers the charm of an imagined first building. Whether it is Robinson Crusoe making his home on a desert island or Thoreau building his Walden in the woods, or whether it is kids making a treehouse or Wendy House in the garden, or whether it is a man hiding out in his garden shed while pretending to work . . . the mini-house, the self-built hut, has proved an extraordinarily resilient trope.

Gaston Bachelard proposed that the spaces we build for ourselves in childhood, from blankets or boxes, beneath our bedsheets or underneath a table, are an echo of the primitive hut, spaces we construct in which to dream. The word 'shed' seems to be etymologically related to the word 'shade'; the shed is a dark dwelling, an oneiric room.

We have our houses, buildings which accommodate the functions and rhythms of everyday life and they are, of course, themselves refuges from the world, but sometimes we need a little bit more. The child's den and the garden shed are attempts to create a separate world within a world, a world over which we have control and the means not only to imagine but to shape. The shed in particular has been picked up in Britain in recent years as a symbol of retreat from mid-life crisis, a traditional bastion of male implements to which they can retreat and gain solace and solitude in a world in which the demands on them appear to be legion. Marcus Berkmann's book *A Shed of One's Own* plays gently on Virginia Woolf's feminist plea for a separate space, defining the shed as a place to potter, a place where men can be left alone. It is intriguing to find that Berkmann has neither garden, nor shed. It is as much a symbolic as a real space, the most easily imagined form of architectural separation within everyday life.

The (real) hut, the shed, the cabin like the den and the cardboard box house are built from the most basic, most elemental of materials, rough-hewn timber, painted, perhaps recycled boards, a hook and eye for a lock and a handle, with the shallow-pitched roof that is so emblematic, the small playhouse windows, square and quartered like all windows should be. Anyone can build one and, unlike the house itself, this is not a space for showing off, for presenting a face to the world, but for retreating into and thinking. And that is how a building intended for the storage of garden tools, or at best for spending an odd night in while out hunting or fishing in the woods, became the *de facto* space of the intellect and of poetic and literary creation.

The list of writers who retreated for their work into their sheds testifies to the disproportionate power of the shabby shack. Heidegger wrote one of the most influential modern analyses of the nature of the house (*Building, Dwelling, Thinking*) in a hut in the Black Forest. George Bernard Shaw wrote in a tiny, but incredible cabin in his St Albans garden. The little timber box was set on a turntable so that it could revolve to follow the path of the sun. Dylan Thomas had a writing shed, so did Virginia Woolf, Mark Twain (an elaborate octagonal folly) and Roald

Dahl. But perhaps Henry David Thoreau's is the most famous of all, because he wrote a book about it, *Walden* (1854). His friend Ralph Waldo Emerson allowed him to build his hut on woods he owned near Concord, Massachusetts and Thoreau's book records the building of the little cabin and concretizes an idea of American self-reliance in the wilderness. That Thoreau's mother brought him baskets of food and that Walden was on the edge of a prosperous town is not allowed to interfere with the narrative. And nor should it. Thoreau's primitive hut served the same function as a garden shed. The issue was one of retreat, not distance. 'Woodshedding' was a jazz term for a retreat into private music, a time away from the scene to concentrate on practice and technique.

The Japanese tea house in paper and timber, despite an elegance which outstrips anything in the limited world of sheds, belongs to the same family, a place where one escapes into ritual and deliberate slowness. So do the follies, belvederes and orangeries in the great gardens and Romantic landscapes of the eighteenth century. The zenith of the whole typology is Marie Antoinette's cluster of fantasy buildings at Versailles: the dairy, the dovecote and the boudoir.

In J.M. Barrie's *Peter Pan* the hero and the Lost Boys build a little shed for the injured Wendy and it is from here the generic term 'Wendy House' entered the English language. Children need to create worlds to escape the adult one within which their lives are so prescribed. Whether it is a shop-bought garden house, a shoddily constructed shack, an appropriated tool shed or a suspect construction of blankets, sheets and clothes pegs, this primal act of making a home is a critical step in the establishing of the nesting instinct. It is the way in which children begin to understand the world of habitation and dwelling in space.

The other brand of shed was placed at the bottom of the garden, at a necessary distance from the house. The outhouse (even its name suggests a miniaturized version of the dwelling) was once a pivotal place, though now it's become a rare thing. Like the shed, the privy was essentially a place of relaxation and escape, a place where a homeowner could sit, perhaps read, certainly think, a place apart. Charles Sale's folksy book *The Specialist* celebrated the craft of Lem Putt, champion privy builder of Sangamon County, who gave advice on the best way to build a privy door.

> 'Now,' I sez, 'how do you want that door to swing? Openin' in or out?' . . . I sez it should open in. This is the way it works out: 'Place yourself in there. The door openin' in, say about forty-five degree. This gives you air and lets the sun beat in. Now, if you hear anybody comin', you can give it a quick shove with your foot and there you are. But if she swings out, where are you? You can't run the risk of havin' her open for air or sun, because if anyone comes, you can't get up off that seat, reach way around and grab 'er without gettin' caught, now can you?'

20 SWIMMING POOLS

WHEN BURT LANCASTER NOTICES that he can see a trail of blue water shimmering in the sunlight between where he is and his house, he begins to swim home. He swims through the pools of friends and neighbours in the New York suburbs in the 1968 film version of John Cheever's *The Swimmer* and, as he does, fragments of his past are slowly revealed. It is an odyssey through the affluent backyard landscape, taking him home and us through his life. Made a year before, Mike Nicholls' *The Graduate* sees Dustin Hoffman's alienated, lost youth floating aimlessly in the sparkling water of his parents' LA pool. For both characters, the pool is a symbol of a kind of ennui – but while Hoffman floats, Lancaster swims, the middle-aged man taking charge of his destiny.

The pool, symbol of a kind of comfortable, wealthy lifestyle from New York to Sydney, manages to be both deeply symbolic and utterly vacuous. One of the most extraordinary, shocking – and now over-used photos in contemporary culture showed a condominium tower in São Paolo with each of the balconies that spiralled down its exterior boasting a pool. Beyond the sparkling water is a view of endless favelas, the rusted corrugated tin roofs creating a landscape of deprivation and desperation hard up against the luxury yet seemingly belonging to another planet.

The vacant, blue-tiled surfaces of pools and their shimmering sparkle has become a universal, an architectural element that stays the same wherever it is. David Hockney's painting *A Bigger Splash* (which dates from the same year as *The Graduate*), with its slick Modernist villa and attenuated palm trees alludes to this world of universalized pleasure. There are no figures, only the eponymous splash indicates the presence of humanity. Freud thought that the appearance in dreams of swimming, and particularly diving, represented sex. Well, of course, he would, wouldn't he? But Hockney's picture, the work of a Yorkshire boy in the blue-skied paradise of California, does suggest Freud was on to something.

If the pool in *The Graduate* represents a suburban dream turned nightmare through the eyes of a younger generation alienated by Vietnam, it could also mean something much darker. 'Nothing' wrote Raymond Chandler, 'ever looks emptier than an empty swimming pool.' Perhaps it is its very potency as a representation of a life of luxury and leisure that can just as easily make it a cipher for all that is corrupt and degenerate. The masterful beginning of Jonathan Glaser's *Sexy Beast* (2000) sees our émigré anti-hero's (Ray Winstone) leathery, sun-tanned paunch all oiled up as he luxuriates in his pool. His peace is disturbed by a huge boulder which rolls down the hillside and smashes into the pool. An even bigger splash. Like an asteroid or shooting star it proves an ill omen, a portent of danger, the dark grey of the London underworld crime come back to haunt his bright, cloudless Mediterranean retirement. And there's nothing new in this appearance of pool as barometer warning of stormy weather. In Henri-Georges Clouzot's *Les Diaboliques* (1955), the wife and mistress dispose of the body of their murdered, abusive headmaster husband/lover in the

119

school pool one dark, wet night. More pit than pool, its muddy water is covered in a carpet of leaves and it becomes a focus for the fear and anxiety of the headmaster's wife, a still-religious former nun riven by guilt her part in (what she thinks was) his murder. The pool recalls the water-filled hole in Poe's *The Pit and the Pendulum* (1842), its darkness a rebuke to the image of the pool as a place of light and breezy leisure. Instead it has become an externalized subconscious, a container of dark secrets. Billy Wilder's *Sunset Boulevard* (1950) opens with a similarly sinister pool. The narrator and hero floats face down – but is filmed from underwater, floating eerily suspended above us, the police photographing him from beyond. 'Poor dope' says the voice-over, 'he always wanted a pool. Well, in the end he got himself a pool, only the price turned out to be a little high.' There is a price to be paid for luxury.

A relatively new development in architecture is the inclusion of pools in big urban houses. Often excavated deep below ground in massive basements they form a kind of dark opposite to the classic Los Angeles pool. If one is about a culture of sun and the healthy outdoors lifestyle fetishized in the inter-war period, the other is an intriguing expression of the fragility of the foundations of our world. Our solid earth is only a thin crust on a core of liquid magma and our earth is supported by a water table so these basement excavations tell a story about a connection to a subterranean realm that is far less solid than we might imagine.

21 ROOFS

A DRAWING BY FRENCH ARCHITECT and theorist Eugène Viollet-le-Duc depicts 'The First Building'. It is the archetypal romantic image of a house in a primitive paradise. Slender saplings still growing from the ground are seen tied together to create a framework whilst Rousseau-esque noble savages begin to clad the structure in what looks like wattle and daub. This is a picture of the house as an organic extension of the landscape, literally growing from the ground and it is an image that has recurred throughout architectural history and one which, with the green movement, continues to inform contemporary building. And it is all roof.

We still refer to having 'a roof over your head', it is synonymous with the idea of shelter, the fundamental element of the dwelling. That 'First Building' has been reflected and refracted into post-rationalizations of all kinds of architecture – the bent boughs have been claimed as the inspiration behind everything from the ribs and vaults of gothic cathedrals to the shaggy haystacks of thatched roofs. These theorizings about the origins of architecture may sound spurious, but if you look at the top of Viollet's primitive hut you'll see a still-living bough protruding from the apex of the roof. That bough has survived into contemporary culture intact. Every major

121

building in Northern Europe and the US goes through some version of the topping out ritual, the most ancient enduring building superstition. The idea is a celebration of the moment the roof reaches its full height – more prosaically also marking the moment builders get to work under cover. There's no definitive version of the mythology behind the ritual – which consists of placing an evergreen tree at the building's highest point and having a celebratory drink – but it is thought to be done to placate the spirits of the trees which have been felled for construction and which dwelt in the woods and landscape now displaced by the building. The evergreen (like the Christmas tree) is also a symbol of growth and good fortune but it also a symbol of man, a kindred vertical being dwelling on the earth – the placing of the tree symbolizes the moment at which the building becomes inhabitable.

For most of the history of architecture, the roof has been, both physically and metaphorically, the zenith of building, whether we are thinking of the domes and attenuated spires of temples or cathedrals, the stacked roofs of a pagoda or a Chinese or Japanese palace, the spiky apex of a French château or the Chrysler Building, the roof is the point at which the building is allowed to meet the sky, to represent the urge to penetrate the heavens. More fantastically it is also often possible to pick up traces of distant myths. The green-tiled roofs of a Chinese palace refer to the scaly back of the dragon which symbolizes Yang: the life force and good fortune, but also power over the extremes of weather, rain, storms, winds. The symbolism was often reinforced in rows of delicately moulded dragons along the ridges. The steep roofs of traditional houses from Norway to Japan refer to the 'world mountain' at the centre of every mythological cosmos, from Olympus and Valhalla to Sinai and Fuji, thus the house becomes a miniature version of the centre of the world, the dwelling place of the gods. In popular culture this has translated into a realm of superheroes. Batman, Spiderman and the rest occupy the neglected zone of the roof, monstrous sentinels looking down upon the city below like animated gargoyles. That filmic, superterranean angle on the city has been amplified in recent years in the predominance of helicopter shots in which the city becomes a landscape of roofs, of air-conditioning units, water-tanks and lift machine rooms not meant for visual consumption, often suggesting a sinister surveillance society. This unsettling angle, the city's new projection has transformed the way we see roofs via Google Earth. We each suddenly have the view of the gods rather than leaving our roofs to pay tribute to them.

The roof is not only the point at which the house meets the heavens but is also itself sculpted by the climate, an earthly reflection of the celestial clouds. Alpine houses echo the spiky peaks of a pine forest, their roofs throwing off the snow, the English thatched cottage is a paean to a fuzzy grey sky, a big cosy muffler; the terracotta-tiled shallow-pitched roofs of a Tuscan village tumble down a hillside like sun-dried, rocky escarpments – and so on. In the city, though, they tend to get a little lost amidst the canyons of walls, as if an increasing detachment from the landscape and an imposed artifice has diminished their existence as an expression of nature and climate. This has combined with a pervasive Modernist attitude of disdain for roofs to a slow, strange disappearance of the most fundamental form in architecture.

It has resulted in the disappearance of arguably the single greatest vehicle for expression of the interior world. Where our houses are now focused on a window, a bay, a view, an opening to the garden, once they were self-contained places, in which the spirit was allowed to rise and expand inside. The stunning joinery of a medieval English roof, the kingposts, crown-posts, hammer-beams are all expressions of wealth, pride in the dwelling and in the craft of the builder. They are creations of a private heaven, a mysterious world above of smoke and shafts of light. Think of that next time you look up at a dropped, white-painted ceiling perforated with a grid of halogen lights. On the other hand you could reasonably argue that our current connections to the heavens, the satellite dishes and aerials that clutter our roofs, are equally symbolic in their cosmic connections.

Some kind of reaction against the blankness of the Modernist flat roof is noticeable, particularly in the work of younger architects. In Switzerland and the Netherlands, architects have been reflecting on the vernacular and suburban traditions of roof, playing with the architectural language, occasionally continuing the materiality of the wall so it embraces the roof (as Herzog & De Meuron and MVRDV have notably done). They seem to have seized on the potential of the roof as a symbol of domesticity and a vital component of the language of home. After years in the symbolic wilderness of Modernism, of being flattened and forgotten, the roof, it appears, is back.

22   FENCES & GATES

'SAM AND CLIFF USED TO BE FRIENDS,' wrote Raymond Carver. 'Then one night they got to drinking. They had words. The next thing, Sam had built a fence and then Cliff built one too.'

The fence, as it appears in Carver's short story 'I Could See the Smallest Things' represents a kind of fall from paradise, the appearance of a symbol of division and tension, the manifestation of wariness and hostility. The word shares its origins, as you might expect, with *defence*, it is a mechanism for keeping the other out. But, as in our era it is usually built from flimsy timber, perhaps only eighteen inches tall – quite easy to just step over – it is also much more than that. The fence is a graphic device, a border, a boundary, a map of the land demarcating private property; it is as close as architecture gets to a pure sign. It has also become an intriguing metaphor for suburbia – the idea of a visual marker dividing endless, seemingly identical plots in a sentimental gesture of possession. When David Lynch wants to introduce us to an archetype of the American dream suburb in *Blue Velvet* (1986) he begins with shots of flowers swaying gently in the breeze against the white canvas of a picket fence. But then, being David Lynch, it all goes wrong. Suburbia, as we now know, is a cipher for a seething hotbed of perversion and vice beneath a veneer of Sunday-best respectability. Dennis Hopper, incidentally, who played the psychotically-crazed Frank Booth in *Blue Velvet*, had his Santa Monica house designed by his friend Frank Gehry. Outside the windowless corrugated metal-clad house he put up a comically inappropriate white picket fence, a good gag which points out the odd symbolism of the fence as sign in a context of urban über-wealth.

The problem however with fences is that they contain and constrict as much as they define. In Carver's world the fence becomes a symbol of alienation, of a world gone bad, just as it does in *It's a Wonderful Life* and *American Beauty*.

Why do we need fences? It is more to delineate than to defend. A world without barriers is also a world of the unknown and the fence is the primal gesture of defining a place, of establishing a private world within the bigger picture. In August Wilson's 1983 play *Fences*, the main character, Troy Maxson, a black former baseball player (and now garbage man) attempts to build a fence around his yard as a defence against the looming prospect of death, convinced its completion will keep him safe. He fails to complete it, and dies. The fence here refers also to the colour bar that stopped him from crossing over into the major league, but it begins to illustrate the power of a pure symbol in contemporary culture. In a very different world, the grimy industrial urbanity of Karel Reisz's *Saturday Night and Sunday Morning*, the fence becomes a constrictive throttle against which Albert Finney's rabble-rousing rebel Arthur Seaton pushes to escape. The fearsome neighbourhood gossips lean on fences as they talk, representing everything the sexually incontinent Seaton is set against. In the film's funniest scene he shoots one of the over-the-fence gossips in the behind with an air gun. Just like the heroes of *It's a Wonderful Life* and *Fences* he fails to escape.

The fence then represents a paradoxical cocktail of security and fear. Its existence is an acknowledgement of the imperfection of the world around us. And as fear escalates, as the super-wealthy and the poor live increasingly side-by-side in contemporary cities, the fence is making the move from the suburban to the urban. But the new fenced settlements are referred to not by the barrier, the fence, but by the euphemism of its opening, the gate. The term 'gated community' is now a commonplace, a euphemism for an anti-urban compound that privatizes streets and alienates the city.

Yet despite this debasement in its usage, the gate remains a potent architectural symbol. The ancients believed that the sun set through a gate at the edge of the world and, after a passage through darkness re-emerged the following day through another. The great monuments and early temples from Stonehenge to Tiwanaku were all forms of sun gate and, as the house is always a manifestation of a mini-temple, the symbolism spread. Just as the sun appears above a door in the rising sun motif of the fanlight, it appears on the suburban Art Deco gate once ubiquitous in British suburbia, a fleeting reference to ancient myth. On grander houses the piers to either side of the gate are a faint memory of the standing stones sun temple just as the wrought iron, forged in fire, echoes in its making the heat of the sun. Just look at Buckingham Palace. The gates are adorned with lions (their fiery manes a symbol of the sun) and highlighted in gold leaf, reflecting the sun's shimmering sparkle. They stand between two stone piers and their swelling profile echoes the aura of a sun rising above the horizon. Going one step better, Sun King Louis XIV is depicted in the gates at Versailles as the sun itself, his flowing locks emanating like rays from his head.

Of course, there are gates to heaven and there are gates to hell, and every gate has two sides, just as the Roman God Janus, deity of beginnings and transitions, had two faces. Janus gave his name not only to January, the first month after the winter solstice and the beginning of a new year but to the 'janitor', who controls the keys and the gates. Janus has passed down to us as St Peter (always pictured in art with a key), controlling heaven's pearly gates, the image of which actually comes to us from a strange description of the New Jerusalem in the Book of Revelation ('And the twelve gates *were* twelve pearls').

What illustrations of the pearly gates make clear is that these are openings in a fence and not a wall. Paradise is visible. A fence can allow both transparency and security but it needs a language with which to convey that message. In the elegant, restrained squares of eighteenth-century London it achieved a subtle, sophisticated vocabulary that allowed it to stay light in weight yet say through a refined language what it needed to. An extraordinary array of finials and decorations emerged, a vocabulary of cast iron elements. There were spears and arrowheads (passive aggressive), urns (classical/tasteful/solemn), acorns (fertile), pineapples (exotic), thistles (Scots) and a huge selection of lights and lanterns for gateposts and corners – a return to the gates of the sun. It's not quite a lost language; designer Matthias Megyeri's 'Sweet Dreams Security' is a witty, unsettling take on the archetype; finials of monstrous, sharp-eared bunnies and sinister penguins present a decidedly contemporary take on the fence as the enduring symbol of domestic security.

23 MINIATURIZATION & REPRESENTATION

I N THE PASSAGE JOUFFROY IN PARIS is a shop that sells every conceivable fitting for a doll's house. There are chandeliers with tiny bulbs like little sparkling diamonds and miniature sundae cups filled with knickerbocker glories. There are decorated Christmas trees and frames in which you can insert sub-postage-stamp-sized versions of masterpieces from the Louvre. There are birthday cakes and chaises longues, Persian rugs and prams, wallpaper and perfume bottles so small the only way to pick them up is with tweezers. Walter Benjamin referred to the Parisian arcades as leftover relics of a golden age of wonder in consumerism, dream houses of desire that dwelt windowless in the middle of Haussmannian blocks like the sub-conscious musings of the urban mind. This shop amplifies that idea of the *passage* as urban dream, a playful window in which you can create new worlds in miniature, worlds that resemble our own yet are wholly unreal – the worlds created by children when they play with dolls houses or model railways, toy soldiers or tanks, worlds in which there are no consequences for actions, and over which (unlike the real world) children can exert control.

But while for children these miniaturized houses represent a finite, playful representation of an incomprehensible whole, for adults there is something ineffably sinister about miniaturization. There is the literary surrealist fear of *Alice's Adventures in*

Wonderland or Gulliver in Lilliput (or yet worse among the giants of Brobdingnag) or of *The Incredible Shrinking Man*, a fear of human-seeming worlds out of scale. The artist Rachel Whiteread made a hobby out of collecting old doll's houses – not the gorgeous unplayed-with type found in country houses, but real toys showing the signs of wear and use that real houses would if they had survived so long with the same décor. Occasionally they are decorated with scaled-down wallpapers or carpets, but more often their walls are papered with the leftover scraps of real wallpaper or wrapping paper, their floors with offcuts of real lino. Whiteread has amassed hundreds and has occasionally piled them into a ghostly miniature village in a dark gallery, illuminated from within but resolutely empty. They are nevertheless filled with real memories and with a psychogeography of play and imagination, their walls distressed with dirt, spots of attic and cellar mould and seemingly miniaturized cobwebs and faded where miniature wardrobes have been placed against walls for decades. Through use and imagination they have become real rooms. Just smaller.

Doll's houses are exactly what children use them for; they are representations of our own houses as we'd like them to be. They are rarely two-up-two-down terraces, but rather stand-alone country houses all built along a front wall so they can be easily played with. They are as much a vitrine for their contents as a representation of as real house, but they are manifestations of an idealized domesticity. As a method of display they are also ruthlessly taxonomic. All the main rooms are represented in order, the dining room, living room, bathroom, bedroom, kitchen, nursery – which usually includes a miniature doll's house. The rooms are only recognisable because of the furniture that is in them, a bedroom is only a bedroom because it has a bed in it, a dining room because it has a table and chairs, a bathroom because it has a bath and so on.

The house is a cabinet for displaying the toys within it, yet it only takes on meaning when it is populated by this miniature furniture. It is the existential emptiness and the anonymity of the bleak spaces that gives Whiteread's village such a chilling effect. It is like when we see a house undergoing demolition (or, far more disturbingly, after bombing or shelling), and suddenly the grimy wallpapers are exposed, or a fireplace or the splintered timbers of the floorboards. A house with its façade removed is profoundly wrong, yet gives us the vicarious tingle of the voyeur, of looking into a private space – just as it is hard to resist peering into illuminated windows from a stationary train to get a snapshot of a moment of real life made more real by its fleeting appearance.

This idea of creating a transparent world through the intervention of the miniature does not stop at doll's houses. There are aquaria with miniature treasure troves and shipwrecks, Mughal-influenced birdcages with mirrors and trapezes, there are the dens that children make for themselves from cardboard boxes and blankets and the Wendy Houses they fill with tea sets. There are Nativity scenes with stables and mangers, model railways executed in astonishing detail populated by hand-painted figures and there are collections of resin houses made for 'collectors' to create entire villages of kitsch, always vernacular, with thatched cottages and Dickensian townhouses, never modern. In fact none of these miniaturized, industrialized products reflects the contemporary. Every doll's house, every model railway and every model village is soaked in nostalgia for the Georgian country house, the bourgeois hotel, the steam railway or the wrecked sailing ship. Miniaturization is in itself a form of nostalgia for a golden age and its natural language is historical. Just as a painted portrait adheres to a moment in time, inevitably the past, the doll's house is a snapshot of a comforting memory, unsuited to modernity.

24 MIRRORS

> 'I'll tell you all my ideas about Looking-glass
> House.' Alice said. 'First, there's the room you can
> see through the glass – that's just the same as our
> drawing room, only the things go the other way. I can
> see all of it when I get upon a chair – all but the bit
> just behind the fireplace. Oh! I do so wish I could see
> *that* bit!'

ALICE IS INTRIGUED, as all children are, by the idea of an alternate reality, another dimension with the mirror as its portal. But she, unlike the rest of us, succeeds in penetrating to the other side.

From *Snow White* and *Dracula* to *The Picture of Dorian Gray* and *The Matrix*, the mirror always tells us something unsettling, whether it is a membrane between ours and another dimension, a dream world or living nightmare or a reflection (or marked lack of reflection) of the uncanny in our own.

Mirrors may not always be embedded in the architecture of home, but they have, over the last five centuries or so, become an integral element in virtually every interior. Venice (the city standing in a lagoon of reflective water) became the centre of a mirror manufacturing monopoly, Murano's glass blowers sparking off a fashion for domestic mirrors that spread through Europe and its new colonies like a plague of shiny convex boils. Its most notable early appearance is probably in Jan van Eyck's symbol-laden Arnolfini Portrait of 1434. The convex mirror appears in the centre of the composition, above a frame created by the conjoined hands of the couple. Perhaps the artist himself is one of the two figures reflected in the mirror, or perhaps they are the witnesses needed to validate the marriage – with Van Eyck's elaborate signature as the documentation. The mirror is surrounded by a frame bearing images of the life of Christ, and indeed the mirror, with its convex iris form, is often seen as a representation of the eye of God.

Mirrors had been convex because they were blown, swelling outwards like a globe, but improvements in glassmaking in the seventeenth century began to allow large flat planes to be made, and the first major architectural expression of these was the Hall of Mirrors in Versailles in 1682. This ceremonial space became an expression of the power of the Sun King, reflecting his royal light, and it remained a pivotal space in which to exert power – the 1919 Treaty of Versailles was signed in the space, the defeated Germans forced to witness their humiliated reflections. The mirrors were a form of architectural theatre, a deliberately dramatic device used to visually double the size of the opulent room and to reflect the sparkle of hundreds of candles burning in chandeliers. From Versailles to Vaudeville, mirrors have been used as architectural spectacle. The Hall of Mirrors at the funfair sees us revelling at the distortions and contortions of our form. The climax of Orson Welles' 1947 film noir *The Lady from Shanghai* takes place in the 'Magic Mirror Maze', a fun house in which shooting the villain is exacerbated by his infinite reflection in the myriad mirrors. It is a scene as surreal and disorienting as is the hall of mirrors for the protagonist – we are never sure exactly what we are looking at, reflection or reality.

Breaking a mirror is, of course, an omen of bad luck, and a reflection distorted and smashed is seen as an indication of a tortured or corrupt soul. This superstitious interpretation of the mirror as reflector of something deeper than mere reality manifests itself in the home at the time of death. During a wake or period of mourning in which the body is present in a room, the mirrors are traditionally veiled. This is partly to prevent the soul from entering the strange netherworld of reflected reality rather than paradise – which is of course the original world of which our realm is only a pale reflection. Partly it is to avoid the soul seeing the body – and attempting to re-enter it rather than heaven. But it is also because the mirror is the symbol of vanity and its covering allows mourners to reflect on the deceased rather than their own appearance.

The first mirror in mythology was the pool that Narcissus peered into and in which he fell in love with his own reflection. All mirrors are a reflection of our narcissism. They congregate in the places we are at our most naked, in the bathroom and the bedroom, above the *vanity* unit. The mirror is the attribute of Venus (often held, as it is in *The Rokeby Venus* by Velasquez, by her son Cupid) but, in its vanity, in the appreciation of beauty it becomes a prelude to lust.

Mirrors also however appear in our more public spaces – our living rooms and parlours. Here the appearance of the mirror – notably as an over-mantle – which became hugely popular in the nineteenth century as a substitute for a painting, is a symbol of the increasing preoccupation with the interior as an expression of the self, of an inner life encapsulated in the possessions and decorations of the room of representation. The mirror becomes

134

a kind of alternative window, not on to the outside world but on to the interior. In London's most infinitely intriguing dwelling, Sir John Soane's House in Lincoln's Inn Fields (1792–1824), the architect used mirrors to increase the complexity of an interior that was already conceived as both museum and mausoleum in his own lifetime. There are mirrors between the windows in the Drawing Room so that the interior can be viewed juxtaposed directly with the world outside, and tiny convex mirrors stud the arches, alcoves and doorways refracting the extraordinary richness of Soane's collections but also bringing in extra light to aid his fading eyesight. The mirror reflects a setting over which we have control – unlike the window, which lets on to a world of unpredictability. It is a window on to the world we build for ourselves, an image of our own interior.

25 PORCHES, VERANDAS & DECKS

T HE WORD VERANDA is one of those wonderful words, like *bungalow*, that come to us from India. It derives from the Sanskrit *varanda*, meaning 'to cover'. But, unusually, it comes to us from two different directions. *Baranda*, in Spanish, is a handrail (the Spanish often mix up Bs and Vs in speech). Portuguese for Veranda meanwhile is *varanda* (the Portuguese, of course, have been in India since Vasco de Gama landed in Kappakadavu in 1498), which takes us all the way back to the beginning.

The veranda is, for the British at least, an exotic word embedded in exotic languages, an architecture that conjures up lazy afternoons out of the searing sun. A gently swaying rocking chair, or perhaps a hammock, and a hat pulled low over the eyes. Perhaps also the casual racism of the American South or the pitiful sight of a young punkawallah fanning his colonial masters. Verandas are the symbol of a colonial life in hot countries. Climate suggests their purpose. These are interstitial spaces between the public and the private realms, places that allow dwellers to be simultaneously at home, under the cover of their own roofs (as the Sanskrit word suggests) and yet still outdoors, enjoying the breeze.

From the simplest porch, a little sloping roof above a door to the most elaborate portico defined by classical columns and a pediment, all these architectural features share the same purpose, to create a zone of ritual preparation for entry and a carefully designated semi-private space.

The word 'porch' derives from 'portico', which was a colonnaded space outside a temple, a covered area that stood before a temple. The most basic porch retains something of that nature, the preparation for and celebration of entry into the private realm. If a veranda might have a rocking chair, a porch might have a trunk or chest, just enough for someone to sit on – perhaps while changing their shoes. It is the remnant of a gesture of hospitality, a seat for an unexpected guest. If the porch is covered it might also house the coats and boots, umbrellas and dog leads which speak of a transition in dress and demeanour from the inside to the outside. The floor material will be different, perhaps with a doormat so that the more delicate surface of the interior is interrupted in preparation for the earth outside. The porchlight hanging above is a symbol of presence, its burning stands for a version of homeliness, the everyday version of a flag flying when the Queen is at home.

If the porch is extended across the front of the house it becomes a veranda. Almost every country and every culture maintains a version of this arcaded space. From the Appalachians to the Alps, Moravia to Malaysia, the veranda exists as a raised deck running the length of the house, quite often the space where a family, particularly the older members will spend more of their waking hours than any other. Even the rooms in Japanese houses, so different in conception, form and material to the more solid and stolid European archetypes, feature a strip of covered wooden decking. In some local traditions porches are so popular they begin to take over the

137

whole façade. Think of the house in *Gone with the Wind* or the curving rear portico of the White House where the porch becomes a balcony for the bedroom floors. On occasion the porch even became the bedroom. On unbearably hot nights it might become a 'sleeping porch' (though my own father relates how as a child he used to sleep on the deck outside his Kent bungalow bedroom even in freezing weather).

The open porch quickly became such an American archetype that landscape architect Andrew Jackson Downing proposed it as the fundamental identity of American building, the thing that differentiated the American house from its English ancestors, a symbol of openness, hospitality, and the conversation and democracy it engendered. He is credited with popularizing the porch for the classes that were moving from city to country as the suburbs exploded as the expansion of the railway network allowed a longer commute. Jackson perceived the porch as a way of reconnecting alienated urban escapees to the landscape and to nature.

That famous front porch hospitality, of course, only went so far. After the end of slavery, black workers, if they needed to converse with the boss man would usually be allowed as far as the porch – the neutral space neither inside nor out, an acceptable but not excessive hospitality. The porch was also the place where children would pick up things about how the world worked, overhearing bits of adult discussions. Nowhere is this better illustrated than in the long hot summer when six-year-old Scout Finch matures during the trial of wrongly accused young black man Tom Robinson in Harper Lee's *To Kill a Mockingbird*. She gets glimpses of trial gossip and explanations from her noble lawyer father but it is the racist reactions of the townsfolk that make her understand the depth of the problem and the weight on her father's shoulders. Scout's neighbour, the mysterious and initially scary Boo Radley (who will eventually be her saviour) arouses her interest. To begin to understand the withdrawn eccentric, she stands on his porch, to try to see his view of the world, to put herself in his shoes. That's what the porch can do, act not only as interface between home and town but between an individual and the world.

26

W E'VE BECOME INURED to the extraordinary thing that happens when we flip a light switch. For almost the entire history of buildings, interiors have relied on the sun for illumination. When the dark descended there was little to do but sleep. The rhythms of life were dictated by the seasons and the sun. Furniture was made moveable so that chairs could be placed by the window to receive the last fading rays of light deep into the evening. For the nights of wealthier householders there were candles, flickering sticks of pale light which were bright enough to ensure the objects in a room were visible but pitifully inadequate for reading, writing, sewing or any of the other tasks which make long, lonely nights interesting.

The wealthy were able to afford dozens of candles in dining rooms and ballrooms, and these cast a particular, delicate light, so the interior fittings were designed specifically to sparkle. Silver candelabra and tableware, walls decorated with mirrors in golden frames, cut glass and polished brass door handles and knobs: objects were intended to pick up the traces of light and refract. Light was something precious, a symbol of status and power. The homes of the poor, if they were illuminated at all, were lit by rushlights – lengths of rush dipped in molten fat and clamped at an angle in an iron holder. To create more light these rushes could be lit from bottom and top – hence 'burning the candle at both ends'. Their light was bright but lasted only 20 minutes or so. One of Aesop's fables, 'The Farthing Rushlight' is a short, odd meditation on their brevity, a story about a rushlight boasting that its light was brighter than that of the sun, the moon and the stars, when a puff of wind from an open door blows it out. Its owner relights it and tells it not to be so proud, saying 'Be content to shine in silence.'

The candle was, of course, also the symbol of divine light. Darkness is seen as ignorance, the flame as enlightenment. In the Jewish tradition the menorah, the seven-armed candelabrum, is the symbol simultaneously of the tree of life, the seven heavens and the light of God. In the early Church, candles were everything. Rites that emerged from the subterranean catacombs, which took place largely after dark to avoid detection, inevitably relied on artificial light and that tradition became engrained in worship. Candles are lit at baptisms, at Christmas and at Easter, for saints and for the dead. Celebration of Mass is inconceivable without a burning light symbolizing the presence of God. The two candles on the altar – which even the Protestants retained despite their distaste at the idea of the symbolic, represent the twin states of Christ – human and divine.

But if the flickering flame represented the light of the divine, the candle also symbolized the fleeting nature of life. In Jan van Eyck's *Arnolfini Portrait* (1434), an elaborate six-armed chandelier hangs from the ceiling between the couple. There are only two candles in it though. The one on the man's side is still burning whilst all that is left of the candle on the woman's side is a few drips of wax and the flame has been extinguished. Perhaps, it has been suggested, this painting (perhaps the best and most symbolically loaded domestic picture we have from the era) was not a celebration of marriage but a commemoration of a death – the wife possibly having died in childbirth (note the way her hand is placed on her belly).

The candle was a representation of humanity as well as divinity – the wax as flesh, the burning wick as soul. Its rich symbolism survives in the reverent way in which candles have become a luxury product, to be used in bathrooms and bedrooms to heighten a sense of pleasure. But their functional life has long been surpassed. First, candles were replaced by gas light, piped into homes from the early nineteenth century. This became an odd interlude, with the new gas supplies being introduced by plumbers – whose expertise in fitting pipes and valves was seen as interchangeable with the requirements of embryonic gas supply. It has left us with the odd situation in which the language of gas supply is coincident with that of water supply, with valves and pipes, taps and mains, flow, pressure and meters. By the mid-nineteenth century, gasoliers had replaced chandeliers as symbols of status and wealth, and householders would draw their curtains and shutters during the day to show off their lamps. The popularity of gas was so short-lived (less than a century) that it barely had time to develop an architectural language – instead building on the existing language of candelabras and sconces, just as it had adopted the language of plumbing. But its replacement, electricity, displayed some intriguing parallels with the symbolism of the candle.

The universally recognized cartoon representation of an idea remains an incandescent light bulb. Somehow this most ubiquitous of fittings attained, in little over a century, the same iconic status as the candle had in millennia. And in many ways, its meaning conveys similar ideas about body and soul, the physical and the mental and about the temporality and fragility of life. The filament burns inside, as blinding as a sun, contained within the vulnerable glass shell that is its only protection. Some lightbulbs in chandeliers imitated candles (some with faux dripping wax running down the side of the lampholder) whilst Modernist designers celebrated the beauty of the bulb itself in fittings which exposed this most exquisite expression of the modern age. Animators and cartoonists were amongst the first to recognize the symbolic significance of the light bulb which quickly became a ubiquitous and instantly recognisable cipher for an idea, a eureka moment. Artist Martin Creed caused a furore when he exhibited a lightbulb switching on and then off again (*Work no. 227*) but you could argue that he was both celebrating the beauty and convenience of a fitting that has become invisible through ubiquity, as well as presenting the lightbulb as metaphor for an idea behind a conceptual work.

We have lost the wonder of electricity and illumination on tap. Nowhere is this more evident than in the banality of electric fittings, particularly the light switch. Here is an interface with an extraordinarily complex system of generation, supply and technology, confined to a white plastic box and the cheapest possible rocker switch. There is no sense of celebration in the action of illumination. It seems odd that we might celebrate our domestic technology in our phones and laptops, our widescreen TVs and massive wireless speakers, yet this most elemental act is ignored. Artificial light has transformed our lives and houses as much as the invention of the chimney did in the medieval era, yet we have become blasé. This has not been helped by the ubiquity of ceilings pocked with halogen lights and the dim, ghostly pallor of energy-saving lamps, neither of which have the clarity or beauty of an incandescent bulb.

27 FLOORS

WHEN DUTCH ARTISTS BEGAN to depict the interiors of their burgeoning bourgeoisie, the humble floor suddenly took on a surprisingly pivotal role in art. It ceased to exist merely as a neutral background, a simulacrum of the earth outside, and instead became a theatrical stage for the subtly unfolding, heavily symbolic episodes portrayed. Pieter de Hooch's *A Boy Bringing Pomegranates* (1662), perfectly shows this complex layering of exquisitely rendered floor finishes, an unfolding of the domestic world portrayed through surface.

The Dutch at around this time effectively invented the modern domestic interior. The combination of the emergence of banking and colonial trade and the wealth they created, allied with a Calvinist sensibility, produced a domestic architecture of incredible refinement. That society was also radically egalitarian. The home, for the first time, became the realm of women and children. De Hooch's subjects were not the epics of myth and religion but the portrayal of domesticity and the paintings were displayed in exactly the kind of dwellings they pictured.

The Calvinist obsession with order, tidiness and cleanliness was reflected in the ubiquity of the tiled floor, scrubbed clean daily not by servants but by the mistress of the house herself.

De Hooch's picture shows first the canal, then the sunlit pavement, then the tiles of an arched entrance, a courtyard and finally the black-and-white tessellations of the interior proper. The gateway marks the threshold between public and private. The terracotta colour of the chequerboard of the courtyard paving marks a private exterior; the earth is represented in the red clay tiles and the man-made artifice of the interior is marked by black and white.

This chequerboard scheme recurs throughout history. It is there in both London's Westminster Abbey and St Paul's Cathedral. It appears in everyday Victorian terraced houses and in the lushest interiors of the Vienna Secession. It is there at the centre of Masonic ritual, representing the floor of Solomon's temple and the idea of the inseparability and inevitable coexistence of darkness and light, good and evil. It is there, presumably for similar reasons, in the nightmarish vignettes of David Lynch and, of course, in the chessboard, where it implies we are but pawns in the great game (for which see also Ingmar Bergman's *The Seventh Seal* in which the knight, our hero, challenges Death to a game of chess).

Paradoxically though, the application of order through a grid imposed on the floor also encapsulates the Enlightenment ideal that mankind can structure the world. The impulse to impose a grid (on the floor or in latitude and longitude) is the same as that which led to the navigation of the globe and Holland's astonishing, if brief, moment as the world's dominant naval and colonial power. The Dutch not only imposed order on the landscape through the imposition of grids, they actually created the land itself. The dykes, canals and polders, reclaimed from the sea, were refined in microcosm in the rigour of the interior.

The stark black and white geometry of the floor needs to be seen as an antidote to what came before it. It can be hard to conceive that for most of human history the default mode of dwelling was the slum and, just as millions still live with dirt floors, the earth itself, compacted and mixed with waste, formed the floors of most European houses. Erasmus wrote of the English floor that it was 'strewn with rushes, under which lies unmolested an ancient collection of beer, grease, fragments of bone, excrement of dogs and cats and everything that is nasty'. This is floor not as representation of an ideal but as a reflection of reality. There is, of course, an easy way to bring order to the chaos – the carpet. The rug is a way of demarcating territory. Whether in a Bedouin tent or a Mongolian yurt, the simple gesture of laying down a carpet on the desert sands or the Central Asian tundra, its positioning on the floor creates a new sense of domesticity and ownership of the particular place. A Muslim's prayer rug, a picnic blanket or a yoga mat indicate the possession of a patch of ground and the temporary transformation of that place into a space of domesticity. This is what, at a larger and infinitely more sophisticated scale, the Japanese do when they proportion their houses to the size and scale of the tatami mat. This rectangular, transportable floor covering becomes the human-scaled module (its proportions a double square) from which the dimensions of the house are built up, so that every element of even the grandest of dwellings is based on the perceptibly human and instantly familiar scale of the mat.

Each material manifestation of the floor is in some way an attempt at ordering the interior world, the chaos and disorder of dirt. Parquet, bare floorboards, carpets and rugs each impose a pattern that dresses the floor as a stage for the choreography of the everyday. Very different, though, was the ancient conception of the floor.

British architect W.R. Lethaby, in his wonderful book *Architecture, Mysticism and Myth* (1891) referred to 'Pavements like the Sea'. His thesis was that for the ancients, the floor was a representation of the primordial waters, the chaos of an as yet unformed world. Look at the mosaic floors of a Roman villa, from Fishbourne in West Sussex to Pompeii, and you will almost invariably see fish, exotic sea creatures and a border of abstracted undulating waves. The floors of palaces and temples were, according to ancient descriptions, of marble so shiny it appeared like the shimmering surface of water or figured in such a way as to imitate ripples and waves. Water always finds its own level, so it becomes the natural metaphor. In modern floors of poured concrete, we see the literal manifestation of a liquid surface made solid.

The Modernist dwelling with its lino and fitted carpets deliberately squeezed this symbolism out. The floor became instead a seamless surface, a bland continuity. There was a deliberate attempt to make the Modernist floor an abstract plane of fanatical cleanliness. This was to be the antidote to the idea of the filthy earth floor, or even the organic warmth of parquet, the obliteration of the idea that the floor might be so directly related to the earth. New materials - lino, terrazzo, polished concrete – emerged to fulfil this desire for reflective purity. They in turn gave way to the muffling neutrality of fitted carpet.

If we return to de Hooch's painting, we can also see a little raised platform on the right, upon which is perched a solitary chair. Because a floor is level, any slight elevation automatically privileges that raised area. Here we see a private space for sitting, probably to catch the light from the window above, perhaps a seat for reading or sewing. This is a miniaturized version of the dais, the elevated floor upon which the king, nobles or master would sit at one end of their great halls. This tradition of an elevated floor is maintained in the Oxbridge colleges, in the 'high tables' reserved for fellows and their guests.

The raising of the floor, the creation of a platform is the simplest possible architectural device, yet it radically alters the character of the room. It seems surprising that so little is done with floors. They are, after all, the stages upon which our lives are acted out.

28   Walls

T HE IDEA OF THE SPIRIT OF THE PLACE or the *genius loci* is a familiar one – that a particular spot, a landscape, a house retains a unique character or atmosphere. But for the Romans this was far from an abstract concept, each place was possessed of an earth spirit and, if the ground was to be disturbed and built on, that spirit needed to be placated so that the building and its inhabitants would enjoy good fortune.

That is what the building sacrifice is all about. The sacrifice of a living thing or an object representing life in the foundations and walls of a house are virtually universal in superstitious societies. At their most terrifying these include myths of immurement and human sacrifice, of wives and children being holed up alive in walls. From extraordinary myths about workmen being immured within the walls of Strasbourg Cathedral to sinister Eastern European legends of wives being built into bridges, their breasts left exposed so they could nurse their babies, the idea of sacrifice was deeply embedded in building culture and myth. It survived the centuries in less grotesque forms through the symbolic slaughter of animals to appease the earth spirits and, often, the incorporation of their bones or even their blood into the mortar and walls. In some societies, stretching from Africa to Greece, builders would attempt to capture a man's shadow as a surrogate for his spirit. Inevitably deemed bad luck, people would be employed to 'look after' their shadow.

These practices later transmuted to incorporate worn shoes or personal tokens, things that had been close to the body, in the structure. Another common gesture was the burying of a coin beneath the threshold or footings. Building works in many Georgian or Victorian houses will reveal some similar token, a memory of building sacrifice. The significance of these gestures has largely been forgotten yet something of them remains in the rituals of laying foundation stones for public buildings and in the burial of time capsules containing personal effects.

The notion of beings built into the walls evokes an idea of the house itself as a thing made alive. The wall is the element which encloses, protects and supports, it is, along with the roof, the most fundamental part of the structure and, in its verticality, it defies gravity, standing tall, just as we do ourselves; it mimics our own life. Whether in the bleeding walls of the movie haunted house, in the wartime slogan that 'walls have ears', in writing appearing mysteriously on the wall or in the built-in expansion joints which acknowledge it as a moving, organic element, walls can seem alive.

Built from brick or stone, the wall is a manifestation of the earth, an extrusion of the materials of the ground to create a man-made cave. Yet their construction also betrays other influences. Gottfried Semper, the Austrian architect and theorist (designer of the magnificent Dresden Opera House), posited that the wall embodies a memory of the woven fabrics of the nomadic tents that enclosed the earliest dwellings. Thus the complex brick bonds are an evocation of the weave of a fabric while the coloured render of a plastered surface, or the wallpaper of an interior, recalls the decorated carpets and hangings that once enclosed us. It is easy to believe if you look at the deep red panels and murals of the villas of Pompeii or the intricate brickwork of a Tudor house, or indeed at the textured wallpapers of the Victorian era. We only now come across flock wallpapers in a few backstreet retro curry houses but flock was once big on walls. As was anaglypta, a moulded wallpaper which gave intricate raised pattering to walls and can still be seen on occasional pub ceilings. These textured wall coverings with repetitive patterns reinforced the idea of wall as tent, evoking the carpeted surfaces of Bedouin tents and central Asian yurts.

But if you look at the arrangement of a traditional wall inside the house you also see something else, the humanizing motif of the tripartite division of the column. Just as the classical column is divided into feet (base), body (shaft) and head (capital), so the wall is split into three by the skirting or dado and the picture rail. We have noted that it reflects the upright posture of the inhabitant and the addition of the dado rail then introduces a uniquely Western line, acknowledging the back of a chair and the sitting position (as opposed to sitting on the floor or squatting prevalent in all other cultures).

Rooms in the Georgian era, when British and North American domestic architecture arguably reached its zenith, were far less fixed in their arrangements than they are today. A writing desk may be moved around near the window to follow the fading shafts of sunlight in the evening; chairs, stools, and chaises longues were moved to the edges of the room to allow bigger social events, harpsichords and games tables migrated from the centre to the edges. The dado rail protected the walls against damage from the backs of chairs as they moved around the room but it also served to break up the mass of the wall and humanize it, giving the room a waist. It was only in the Victorian era, with the introduction of chunky furniture and later with the three piece suite and, particularly, the TV that rooms began to settle into more permanent patterns of usage. Intriguingly, the laptop and wireless may begin to lighten up the room taking us back towards more flexible patterns of usage.

That the wall is our fundamental measure of normality, of comfort and containment is testified by phrases including 'off the wall', 'driving me up the wall' and so on. It is also extraordinarily rich in evocation – it can represent the boundaries of a great city or the fabric of a tent, the basketwork web of medieval wattle and daub or the perfectly-proportioned container of a classical temple, it is as much a canvas depicting the memory of dwelling as it is an envelope with which we happily confine ourselves. But the wall is also a memory machine. Our walls are filled with the images that are dear to us. There are paintings and photos, flatscreens and mirrors reflecting our own faces; there are brackets and shelves, clocks and books, a mapping of our existence in the physical world of objects and images. Occasionally this idea of the wall as mental map can go awry. The walls of Sir John Soane's House in London's Lincoln's Inn Fields present an archaeology of the mind of an architect, a taxonomy of history and myth, symbol and death. They are decorated with the fragments of antiquity and the art of a modernity, which at that moment was captivated by Pompeii and the oppressing idea of a civilization immeasurably greater than that on show in contemporary London. The wall was a reminder of the inadequacy of the contemporary. In other instances the wall can be made into a cross between a fortification intended to keep the outside outside and a padded cell to protect the inhabitant form himself. There was Proust, who lined his bedroom with cork to protect himself from the noise of the outside world and to act as a sponge to absorb the city's grime and the dust that exacerbated his asthma. The cork was the insulation from the city, which allowed him to turn inward and concentrate on his reminiscences and create *Remembrances of Things Past*. It is similarly a trope of film to represent a twisted villain or tortured soul through the creation of a room clad in pictures or crucifixes, newspaper articles or pages from books, attempts to turn the wall into an incantation against the thing that afflicts or obsesses. There is the priest's room in *The Omen*, plastered in pages from the bible to protect him from the sins of the past but there are also the bleeding walls of *The Amityville Horror*.

It was that richness of meaning and history that led Modernist architects to attempt to dispense with it as far as they could. In their efforts to create a new architecture free of memory (or, as they saw it, constraint), they replaced solid walls with glass, internal divisions with fluid space, rooms with flowing plans. Frank Lloyd Wright, in his characteristically eccentric manner, associated corners with fascism, so got rid of them as far as he could. Others went one step further. Houses like Philip Johnson's Glass House (New Canaan, Connecticut, 1949) and Mies van der Rohe's Farnsworth House (Plano, Illinois, 1951) attempted to dispense with walls altogether. Both conceived as summer houses, they demonstrate the ethereality of wall-less living but also its oddness. They feel insecure, insubstantial; they provide no embrace or enclosure; they remain sophisticated, beautiful gazebos. Where Modernist architects did need to retain walls, the bathrooms or the kitchens for example, they tiled them. Tiles represent a measure of control, they inscribe an abstract grid on the wall, they map it. Just as the creation of maps with their carefully measured grids imposed ownership on a piece of land, a grid of tiles inscribes ownership on a wall. The clean joints and edges, the easy-to-wipe glossy surface is a denial of the rough nature of the construction beneath, the earthy bricks and irregular mortar, the materials smelling of their connection to the earth and the underground. To tile is to impose order.

But the wall, despite the best efforts of the finest architects and engineers, remains far too deeply embedded in our consciousness to just disappear. Flann O'Brien, the brilliant Irish satirist, parodied ideas of dispensing with walls in his unsettling novel *The Third Policeman*. The book's narrator is obsessed with the writing of useless philosopher and polymath, De Selby. De Selby's eccentric views included a visceral dislike of walls. 'Evidently', O'Brien writes 'his main objection was to the confinement of a roof and four walls. He ascribed somewhat far-fetched therapeutic values – chiefly pulmonary – to certain structures of his own design, which he called 'habitats'. These 'crude designs' had 'the conventional slate roof but no walls save one, which was to be erected in the quarter of the prevailing wind; around the sides were the inevitable tarpaulins loosely wound on rollers suspended from gutters on the roof . . . In the light of present-day theories of housing and hygiene, there can be no doubt that de Selby was much mistaken in these ideas but in his own remote day more than one sick person lost his life in an ill-advised quest for health in these fantastic dwellings.' All of which is why, of course, we still –despite the efforts of Modernists and fictional philosophers – have walls.

29   CORRIDORS

Privacy is a relatively recent idea. For most of the history of homes, space was shared with families, friends, servants, guests and animals. Even when rudimentary bedrooms finally arrived to supplement the great halls of the medieval era, these were public spaces. Dressing, receiving guests, bathing would all be done around a retinue of others. If there was any privacy it might be achieved in a study or a library or through the wrap-around curtains of a double bed. The grand mansions of seventeenth century Paris, the *hôtels* which became the model for sophisticated urban living, were always designed with grand vistas rather than cosy nooks in mind. The effect was a theatrical enfilade, a row of rooms opening on from each other, their double doors perfectly lined up so that a guest could see from one end of the house to the other in a dramatic single perspective. It meant, however, that to get to any room entailed a journey through other rooms.

Continental European apartments often retained this idea of the grand enfilade right through until the early twentieth century (anywhere from Berlin to Budapest you'll often see a bourgeois central European apartment with three huge rooms opening into each other) just as you can see the same dramatic sequence in English country houses with their endless galleries and chambers. But in the cities changing perceptions of private life combined with fast-rising property prices had begun to inform a new architecture which saw taller, tighter terraces of houses being built as a suite of separate rooms accessed off a central stair via landings. The German observer Hermann Muthesius suggested that the English desire for privacy, for retreat from the bustle of the city streets, was the same impulse that drove them to abandon the rooms with communicating doors still popular in his homeland.

In bigger houses these landings became attenuated into corridors, which allowed residents and guests to reach individual rooms from dedicated circulation space. In functional terms it also allowed the development of houses tightly squeezed on to thin slivers of urban land – the longer and thinner the site, the longer and narrower the corridor. This was a major transformation as rooms began to take on distinct and discreet characteristics and dark hallways (the windows were usually in the rooms to either side) became a feature of domestic space. The hierarchy of house plans became increasingly complex and corridors and passages proliferated.

That complexity began to echo the qualities of the labyrinth. The original labyrinth was beneath the Palace of Knossos, a dark space built by the royal architect Daedalus to confine the half-man, half-bull Minotaur. Theseus kills the Minotaur and is able to escape through tracing his steps back the way he came via a thread given to him by Ariadne – that thread was called a 'clew', or 'clue' – which leads him out of the darkness. In medieval times the labyrinth and the maze were adopted by monks and mystics as a device to disorientate, to disconnect the body from the world around it and allow the mind to concentrate on higher matters. The corridor – dark and separate from the rooms it serves – retains that sense of the unknown, a place not of itself but a path to be travelled.

There is something unsettling about a long corridor with closed doors leading off it. Its length and narrowness appears to accentuate the perspective. The most extreme versions can be found in hotels where things – trays of food, shoes, newspapers – mysteriously appear and disappear outside the rooms without doors ever seeming to open or close. Perhaps this is why the endless corridor became such a trope of both horror and surrealism. In *The Omen* (1976) young Damien seems to be compelled by the perspective of the corridor to pedal his trike faster and faster until he knocks his (surrogate) mother off the landing forcing her to miscarry. In Stanley Kubrick's *The Shining* (1980), the corridor of an empty, off-season hotel becomes a space of haunting and terror for the small child, while in Jean Cocteau's *La Belle et La Bête* (1946) the eponymous beauty is drawn down a strange, lavish but surreal corridor in which the arm-shaped wall sconces follow her passage. In the Coen Brothers' *Barton Fink* (1991), a terrifyingly infinite hotel corridor remains completely lifeless and uninhabited yet shoes still appear outside rooms each evening, as if by magic. This was the space of anonymity. Other endless corridors appear in Terry Gilliam's *Brazil* (1985) and Adrian Lyne's *Jacob's Ladder* (1990) as symbols of a descent into a nightmarish netherworld. In horror the corridor virtually gets a category of its own, from Hammer Horror's *Corridors of Blood* (1958) to the South Korean film *Whispering Corridors* (1998) and from *The Corridor* (2010) to *Shock Corridor* (1963), this most seemingly neutral of spaces is in fact a staple.

From its simple roots as a mechanism for maintaining privacy, the corridor came to symbolize a lifeless, even sinister, liminal zone. Its adoption in institutions – hospitals, hotels, bureaucracies and so on hopelessly tainted its image. What became known in Victorian and Edwardian houses rather grandly as 'the hall' was in fact a corridor, a mongrel mix of cloakroom, accessway and stairwell, its obligatory accessory a console table too weak and thin to stand up on its own and leaning against the wall. This uncomfortable location, it is now almost difficult to remember – the public space that was there to provide privacy to the rooms – was once the location of the family phone, a place where everyone could hear everything so that the most private means of communication became the most public.

The corridor represented everything modern architecture was against: mean, dark, dusty and ill-defined. From the late nineteenth century, British architects began to do away with corridors, replacing them with generous lobbies and flowing spaces and by the mid-century corridors had disappeared from Modernist houses replaced by fluid, open plans. Those burdened with older houses took sledgehammers to their walls, knocking-through to create poor-men's versions of Modernist villas.

The corridor has never been a desirable feature; instead it is a space created by necessity. Neither has it ever been a space in which one dwells, instead it is a place of transition between spaces. In one way, that combination of anonymity, necessity and a feeling of unease about its spatial awkwardness has laid it open to a generalized feeling not only of unease but also of farce. It is the place of unintended meetings between inhabitants of otherwise closed doors. The classic bedroom farce in which errant partners meet in corridors whilst desperately trying to avoid each other is a theatrical cliché but it has also become a staple of film. From *Yellow Submarine* to *The*

Pink Panther, the corridor is depicted as a place of confusion and embarrassment. The niggling fear of being trapped in a semi-public corridor, locked out of your room, becomes the acme of humiliation. The constant opening of doors and entering of the wrong rooms, the accidental meetings and couplings created by the serendipity of the wrong door, the slapstick potential of outward opening doors and so on have all combined to make the corridor an odd blend of fear and farce, a disturbingly charged space which means much more than it seems.

30

CEILINGS

WHEN A CEILING COLLAPSED last year in Rome it seemed to be just another story of municipal neglect. A big chunk of the ceiling (the house is now buried below the next Roman layer, Hadrian's Baths) fell in due to rainwater damage, but the story faded from the headlines as quickly as it arrived. This ceiling had crowned one of the most extraordinary houses ever built, the Emperor Nero's Domus Aurea, his Golden Palace. What we know of Roman ceilings is what has survived in places like Herculaneum and Pompeii; elsewhere it is mostly walls and floors that remain. But we know about Nero's ceilings because Suetonius described them in *The Lives of the Twelve Caesars*.

'The supper rooms were vaulted', he wrote 'and compartments of the ceilings, inlaid with ivory, were made to revolve, and scatter flowers, while they contained pipes which shed unguents upon the guests. The chief banqueting room was circular, and revolved perpetually, night and day, in imitation of the motion of the celestial bodies.'

Nero's ceilings, like all of our ceilings, were representations of the heavens. The dining room ceiling was apparently painted blue and decorated with stars and could be retracted so that guests could dine under the stars. This is the most literal execution of the idea of the ceiling as sky, which also explains its etymology – from the French *ciel*, or sky. The conflation also, critically, works the other way around. Hamlet, in his 'What a piece of work is man' monologue talks of the heavens as 'This majestical roof fretted with golden fire'. The sky itself was seen as a dome, a vault or a ceiling, a canopy either pierced to reveal pinhole glimpses into a heaven of blinding light or studded with sparkling gems. The vaults of the medieval cathedrals, now so dour and grey in their stripped stone, were once painted in blue and decorated with dozens of golden stars and suns. In the Renaissance, ceilings of palazzi were daubed with clouds and angels, with mythical scenes and allegorical and astronomical mappings. Ceiling paintings across Europe and South America depicted figures drawing curtains aside to reveal the heavens, *putti* perching on fluffy clouds, perhaps even, as at the Sistine Chapel, the creating hand of God Himself. All this was framed in intricate gilded carvings or gesso work as the ceiling became a picture of the sky above, both visible and invisible, the skies of life and of the afterlife.

Even the debased mass-produced houses of the Victorian era unconsciously carried the accumulated meaning of millennia in their complex collections of mouldings and ceiling roses. And they all kept the frame. We may not see much meaning in it now, in the mean cornice decorations that house-builders wrap around the junctions of wall and ceiling but these are the remnants of the framing of the heavens.

Those mouldings, now abstracted into simple decorative tropes, also celebrate the meeting of the wall and the ceiling, they bring our eyes to what architecture is all about. A house is a roof – which is expressed internally as a ceiling – and the walls that support it. Architecture is essentially all about how the two are joined together, a celebration of structure. That idea of the ceiling as a representation of structure itself means that the effects of any imperfections are felt disproportionately. In the Coen brothers' *Barton Fink* (1991), the luckless writer looks up from his bed at the ceiling of his seedy hotel and notices the spreading water stains, which become the perfect metaphor for the collapse of his dreams. In Roman Polanski's *Repulsion* (1965), the ceilings begin to crack as a symbol of Catherine Deneuve's breakdown whilst slowly spinning ceiling fans in films from *Blade Runner* to *Angel Heart* portend doom, a bladed barrier to a soul moving towards heaven. On the other hand, Pop artist Richard Hamilton's wonderful work *Just what is it that makes today's homes so different, so appealing?* (1956) sees its collaged domestic interior crowned by what looks at first like a close up of the moon's surface but turns out in fact to be a satellite picture of the earth hanging in the heavens in an intriguing reversal of the usual duality of earth below and heavens above.

It's certainly possible to think that the contemporary home has abandoned any notion of the ceiling as a symbolic element. We most frequently encounter a flat white plane devoid of any ornamentation except perhaps those mass-produced cornices at its edges. The ceiling has become something better ignored, a surface to reflect light back down into the room. But in fact the remnants of its symbolic purpose proliferate. The chandeliers which spread through the palaces of eighteenth century Europe and which still form the centrepiece of many grand domestic spaces are symbols of the stars, the twinkling lights of a fiery firmament. They are derived from medieval candelabras, which were suspended from the ceiling on two pieces of wood jointed together in the shape of a cross with one candle on each arm, the religious symbolism of Christ as the light of the world made manifest. The ceiling itself celebrates the light – the ceiling rose is an irruption of decoration around the chain or cable. After the introduction of gas lighting, ceiling roses grew to become huge decorative elements concealing vents through which gas fumes could escape via ceiling ducts.

Later light fittings, including the glass globes which were common in the early Modernist era, refer to the sun: a suspended, illuminated ball. Then there are the dropped ceilings which have now become the industry standard with their grid of halogen spots. What are these if not an attempt to recapture something of the evenness of a bright sky combined with the dimmed spectacle of a sky full of stars?

Then, of course, just as in Nero's palace, there are the skylights, windows to the heavens, which begin to bring the sky down into the interior. In bedrooms, bathrooms, places of recline skylights give the illusion of release, of infinity stretching above – even if city lights, condensation, dust, dirt, leaves and clouds may obscure everything you could possibly have seen. This might, if we were feeling a little morbid, remind us that the stars, unlike us, seem eternal. When the pharaohs were buried not only were the ceilings of their burial chambers in the pyramids inscribed with myriad stars, but the undersides of the lids of their coffins were painted blue and decorated with golden stars. If the floor anchors us on earth, the ceiling allows our spirits to aspire to the sky.

31 STUDIES & LIBRARIES

ONE OF THE MOST CURIOUS yet most influential interiors in the history of art is the painting of *St Jerome in his Study* by Antonello da Messina (*c*.1430–79) in the National Gallery in London. It depicts the saint in his study, but it is not the kind of room we would recognize, in fact it is not really a study at all. Rather the painter depicts the saint on a raised dais, four steps above the level of the tiled floor. It is an intriguing construction which sits in a much larger space, a grand and complex set of volumes which suggest a church or a monastery. There is a vault on the right supported on a row of slender Renaissance columns, on the left a window with two simple window seats, each looking onto a classic northern Italian landscape of rolling hills punctuated with cypresses. The whole is an extremely carefully constructed composition within a *trompe l'oeil* frame within the picture frame. Perspective was still a relatively new device and the artist uses it to full effect to create a theatrical scene with the saint on his stage and the stone frame through which the picture is viewed as a proscenium arch. The perspective lines do not converge as you might expect on the saint himself but on the book in front of him. The brilliant white of its pages seems to seep off the surface through his pale hands and up into his face, while the distance between him and his book is bridged by another volume leaning at a slanting angle on the shelf behind him.

There are a number of intriguing devices here which reveal much about the techniques of Renaissance composition and symbolism, but which also illuminate the way a study is perceived, what this most cerebral of rooms means.

Its elevation on that stage is both practical and symbolic. The stone or tiled floors of unheated buildings would have allowed the cold to be drawn into the human body. Raising the study a few steps on a timber floor would have reduced the effects of the cold. Note that he has left his shoes at the bottom of the steps, in the way one might remove them to enter a temple (or if his feet were no longer cold). But this lifting of the room within the room also indicates that this is a place of elevation through learning, that the mind and the soul are symbolically raised by the process of engagement with books. Interestingly, the books on the shelves do not appear with their spines outwards as we might expect but are placed as if on exhibition, opened for us to see. Perhaps this is to illustrate that the value in books lies not in their appearance as status symbols on a shelf but in the words contained within them.

This study might be on show to us but it is not a public space, but a resolutely private one. The saint has constructed his own world within the bigger building and is surrounded by the objects that define his existence. The other items on the right of the shelf – pots, plates, jars – are to do with everyday existence. One vessel sits precariously atop the shelf seemingly about the drop, a commonly used trope indicating the impermanence and uncertainty of life which the Dutch still life painters would pick up on a couple of centuries later.

Then there are the animals, the cat on the left (which has found itself a spot on the warmer dais) and a lion in shadow on the right, the one from whose paw St Jerome famously pulled a thorn. The peacock symbolizes the immortality of the saint and of the word of God which he translated.

Albrecht Dürer's engraving of *St Jerome in His Study* (1514) shows a study curiously bereft of books (only a few appear, rather rigidly on the far left) and which is instead dominated by a self-satisfied lion and the gleaming pate and halo of the elderly saint. Here, the signs of the vanity of objects and possessions are even clearer. The skull on the window sill and the huge hour glass hanging ominously behind the saint are the classic memento mori. Knowledge, it says, lasts longer than the lifespan of a single man. Here too it is clear that this is a privileged place, guarded by a lion and a dog, the precious light streaming in, the chairs which were still a new and luxurious piece of furniture.

The study remains, even in our houses today, a privileged space in the midst of the practicalities of everyday life, a place to escape domesticity into a world of words and writing. It occupies a curious position between work and leisure. There is a luxury in having a dedicated study but it is one tempered by its presence as a reminder of the weight of work lurking around the corner. It is this dichotomy between the pleasure of retreat into a world of books and the heavy conscience that there is always work you should be doing that is critical in the often poorly understood difference between a study and a library.

In his beautiful book *The Library at Night* (2006), Alberto Manguel is careful to make this distinction. He describes the tendency to conflate the study and the library, yet thoughtfully separates the two when he builds his own house. The study, Manguel asserts, is always freighted with the associations of work. It may be a room enclosed completely in books, but it is a place of writing and reading for writing. This distinction might appear ludicrous to anyone crammed into a tiny apartment or who isn't a writer/academic in the Manguel mould, but he makes an important semantic distinction. The library, as opposed to the study, is a place of pleasure, in which the reader can escape into books for no reason other than enjoyment. For Manguel, it is a place that is at its most intense at night, when the house is quiet and when the pools of light that form on the tables beneath the study lamps provide a secondary spatial experience within the bigger room, creating both intimacy and focus.

The rise of the home office, the ability to work in a networked way, at home yet connected to the world, has brought the study back into the house but, at the same time, the ubiquity of the laptop and Wi-Fi and the diminution of the role and value of books has led to a dissolving of the room's role into the dwelling as a whole. A strange thing has happened to studies – look at any book of interiors or tips for how to arrange your home and you will find pieces on how to situate a home office beneath the stairs, or perhaps in a bit of left-over space off the hall or on the upstairs landing. Otherwise you may see schemes envisaging a kind of cupboard as a home workspace, or systems of screens allowing a bit of your bedroom to be used without disrupting your daily routine. This kind of thing is fine for a small apartment where space is valuable and rare but it is quite another thing to find similar solutions suggested for big houses with generous floorplates, whether the UK's horrible executive housing or the US's massive McMansions.

If people are going to be increasingly working from home (or perhaps rather working in their own leisure time from home) then a study is not a luxury but a necessity as it allows a proper delineation of labour and domesticity. Once you shut the door, you are free.

The study is the space of wisdom and learning, to lose it is to delegate knowledge, to collapse the real space of inherited meaning and symbolism into the ether of cyber space and to make the whole home a place of work.

32   CHRISTMAS

MORE THAN ANY OTHER TIME, Christmas focuses the mind on the home and the hearth. Partly because it feels right – the domestic is the default setting of the holiday, but partly because that is how we have been conditioned. In literature, film, TV and advertising, Christmas has become the symbol of domestic bliss or of its absence. In Dickens' 1843 *A Christmas Carol* (the book that effectively instigated our version of the holiday), Ebenezer Scrooge's large, miserable house becomes the embodiment of his meanness and lack of humanity, a home for a lost soul. Dickens describes it as

> a gloomy suite of rooms, in a lowering pile of
> building up a yard, where it had so little business
> to be, that one could scarcely help fancying it must
> have run there when it was a young house, playing at
> hide-and-seek with other houses, and forgotten the
> way out again. It was old enough now, and dreary
> enough, for nobody lived in it but Scrooge, the other
> rooms being all let out as offices. The yard was so
> dark that even Scrooge, who knew its every stone,
> was fain to grope with his hands. The fog and frost
> so hung about the black old gateway of the house,

that it seemed as if the Genius of the Weather sat in mournful meditation on the threshold.

When Marley's ghost manifests himself it is on the lion-head doorknocker, engraining himself in the fabric of a house that once belonged to him. Scrooge's house is contrasted with the humanity, the steam, warmth and cooking smells of Bob Cratchit's measly home and the festive luxury of his nephew Harry's home, a place of fun and games. Scrooge's house is dark ('Darkness', writes Dickens 'is cheap, and Scrooge liked it.'). But when he is visited by the Ghost of Christmas Present, his bedroom is transformed.

> The walls and ceiling were so hung with living green, that it looked a perfect grove; from every part of which, bright gleaming berries glistened. The crisp leaves of holly, mistletoe, and ivy reflected back the light, as if so many little mirrors had been scattered there; and such a mighty blaze went roaring up the chimney, as that dull petrifaction of a hearth had never known in Scrooge's time, or Marley's, or for many and many a winter season gone.

And that, symbolically at least, is what we try to do to our homes at Christmas, to banish the atmosphere of the everyday in favour of an enhanced domesticity. The story of the Christmas tree is familiar, but it is worth remembering that the evergreen is an extremely symbolic element, a living thing sacrificed to bless the house in a reminder of a tradition which is truly amongst the oldest memories in the home – trees and boughs are still installed on a roof in a ceremony to celebrate 'topping out' or the completion of a roof in construction, the weatherproofing of a house. The bringing in of a Christmas tree is an equivalent act but it is also something that signifies the end of winter, a piece of green which has survived intact and the candles, the glittering balls and, more recently, the fairy lights upon it, are the celebration of the light coming anew to the world outside. The star at its top is not only a hint at the star over Bethlehem but also of the sun itself, crowning the whole event. In fact, the Nativity, and the little scenes recreated with manger and figures, serve to reinforce the domestic nature of Christmas through its narrative of homelessness, of Christ having been born in a stable.

Virtually every successful Christmas staple since Dickens has treated the house and home as an embodiment of an idea of wellbeing, and its disturbance as an aberration – a signifier of all that can go wrong. In Frank Capra's *It's a Wonderful Life* (1946), we are deeply unsettled by James Stewart's everyman George Bailey's discomfort at home, riled by the noise, the music and the baluster globe which comes off in his hand every time he ascends the stairs. He shouts and suffers, effectively, a suicidal nervous breakdown. Of course, everything is saved by an angel (as he saves the angel from drowning) and all is made good again in the house at the end, beside the Christmas tree. In *Home Alone* (1990), eight-year-old Kevin is accidentally left behind to defend a house against intruders, and the house itself becomes a protagonist, a weapon used against the bungling burglars but again, the unsettling notion of a child alone at Christmas is embodied in the family home itself, huge and empty. In *Miracle on 34th Street* the connection is made even clearer when only child of a single mother, six-year-old Susan (Natalie Wood in the 1947 original), challenges Kris Kringle to make her believe he really is Santa Claus by asking for a family and a house. At the end she is given exactly that, a house to precisely match the one she drew. The house becomes, once again, the embodiment of family and domestic happiness. That immediate post-War era seemed, perhaps unsurprisingly, to bring out a certain sentimentality in the idea of Christmas as an idealized family holiday.

Miracle on 34th Street, with its drunken fake Santa at the root of the real Father Christmas's problems (foreshadowing Billy Bob Thornton's *Bad Santa*), brings out a little of the strange symbolism of the Santa story. An old man descending the chimney to bring gifts? It's an almost sinister mythology (one played upon so brilliantly by Tim Burton in *A Nightmare before Christmas* which conflates Halloween horror with Christmas cheer). It has strange roots. St Nicholas, the original Santa Claus, was Greek, but born in modern-day Turkey (though his remains were stolen and taken to Bari). One legend recites a story of a famine, during which a butcher has murdered three young boys to make ham and stored them in a barrel, from where they are rescued and resurrected by St Nicholas. Another version has him taking pity on three young girls who, lacking a dowry, are likely to be forced into prostitution and St Nicholas anonymously gives them gifts of gold coins, dropped into freshly washed stockings left hanging on the window to dry. A further version yet has him clambering onto a roof so as not to be detected and dropping gold into the embers in the hearth. In much of Europe St Nicholas still comes on his feast day, 6 December, and deposits gifts of sweets, nuts, tangerines and gold chocolate coins in shoes or boots left by the window. Elsewhere, it is the hearth that remains the focus. The fire inside is delightful, with all those roasting chestnuts, but it is the symbolism of warmth and light that makes it so central. Thus the mantelpiece becomes the domain of Christmas cards and swags of green, a combo in which the primeval forest is both celebrated (holly, ivy, mistletoe and paper) and transformed (the log or coal fire). The odd symbolism of a Santa descending the chimney (listen to Eartha Kitt's 'Santa Baby': 'hurry down the chimney tonight') reminds us of the festival as a turning point in the cycle of the seasons, the return of fertility.

If the idea of an (albeit benevolent) intruder is a little unsettling, another odd facet of the feast is a tendency to miniaturize. Whether in the reduced figures of a nativity scene, the shrunken toys and baubles suspended from a Christmas tree or topping a Christmas cake, or in the atrophied scale of decorations for a dolls house, the tiny pictures at the windows of an Advent calendar or the miniature Christmas scenes which tend to light up creating tiny illuminated, snow-covered, hyper-Dickensian townscapes, there is a sense of wanting to create miniature Christmas worlds. Clement Clarke Moore's 1823 Santa Claus is still a 'jolly old elf', his reindeer 'tiny', not the rotund giant we think of – who bears more resemblance to Dickens' Dionysian ghost of Christmas Present. Perhaps this miniaturizing is a way of creating a cosy, controlled, ideally domestic world. Like Christmas decorations themselves, it is about a transformation, an illumination, the retrieving of half-forgotten things from boxes in dark, dusty attics and cupboards and bringing them out to sparkle. The miniaturization is an attempt to create the ideal Christmas world we have come to expect from an overwhelming mythology of literature, film and advertising. And it is easier to create at a tiny scale when everything can be perfect.

33 Columns & Pillars

COLUMNS, YOU MIGHT THINK, are for the grandest houses only, for the porches of colonial mansions or Georgian country houses. But in fact their ubiquity has made them almost invisible. Once you start looking, they're everywhere. Their association with grandeur, with temples and palaces, with classical civilization and imperial pomp and, most particularly, with wealth and status, has made the column a recurring and indefatigable symbol. They are the DIY add-on part excellence. They can be found on porches and around entrances (my apartment block has a particularly squat and bulging pair guarding its flanks). They appear between rooms, on cupboards and armoires, as candlesticks and as garden ornaments, in grander halls and as newel posts and, of course, where walls have been removed or opening widened.

Perhaps the survival of this most tenacious of architectural archetypes has something to do with its deep associations with both the tree of life and our own bodies. We are all supported ourselves by a spinal column and our erect being in the world, the stature which marks us apart from the animals, is the same verticality expressed in a structural column.

The tree of life is one of the fundamental archetypes of mankind, a symbol of stability, fertility, growth – both physical and spiritual – and a model for the cosmos. Virtually every cosmology and religious mythology features a tree at its centre. There are trees supporting the world in their branches (the Norse Yggdrasil) and trees as *axes mundi* (like the cosmic tree beneath which the Buddha attained enlightenment and in imitation of which pagodas and stupas are erected). There are transformational trees (like the one that the goddess Daphne turned into to avoid the advances of Apollo) and trees of knowledge (as in the Kabbalah and also the tree from which Eve picked the apple). There are trees of sacrifice (the wood of the crucifix) and trees of ascent (mythical trees climbed in trance by a shaman) and there are trees of fertility (like the myrrh tree from which Adonis was born or those represented by May poles). And all these trees have come to be represented in architecture, the roots of which are in wood.

In the eighteenth century there was an explosion in speculation about where architecture came from, about the primitive state of pure dwelling, a question about where Rousseau's noble savage might have lived. The myriad suggestions converged on a hut made from raw tree trunks and a shallow pitched roof of branches looking surprisingly like a Greek temple. The idea was to demonstrate that the rules of classical architecture were derived and abstracted from nature, from the source. Look at the capital of a Corinthian column and you can see the acanthus leaves scrolling out, as they do on a composite capital. Egyptian columns had capitals of abstracted lotus and papyrus leaves. In gothic cathedrals and Mannerist palazzi, columns often appeared as rough-hewn trunks carved in stone, an artifice which reinforces the memory of the tree in all structure. Trees remind us of ourselves. Jung asserted that the tree was a symbol of the self-depicted as a process of growth. In this way, columns also become representations of ourselves, architecture made human. In the most literal instance this leads to caryatids, the female figures carved as columns. The Karyatides were the priestesses of Artemis at Caryae, immortalized in stone. But more subtly the other orders also represent the human body. The Doric is male, stout and sturdy, the diameter of its base one sixth of its height, its shaft scalloped and muscular. The Ionic meanwhile has a base diameter one eighth of its height, and its slenderness suggests a female form, as do the Princess Leia buns to either side of its capital and the delicate fluting of the shaft, which is intended to represent the folds of the fabric of a dress. Columns have character, and when they are stretched out of shape, too fat, we can tell.

One architect in particular made a fetish out of the column and created an entire language out of his endless, inventive variations. The Slovenian architect Joze Plečnik began his career in Vienna and Prague but returned home to Ljubljana to help create the infrastructure of a new capital city. Everything from lamp posts to mausolea was defined by the eccentric inclusion of columns, often placed singly and centrally where their very human characteristics come to the fore. His work with columns has never been bettered.

Among the most curious of dwellings were columns themselves. Simeon Stylites the Elder took up his position atop a column in Syria in 423 and stayed there till he died thirty-seven years later. It started something of a trend. For centuries, hermits, ascetics and oddballs would live on tiny platforms on columns, certainly feeling elevated above the everyday, perhaps feeling closer to heaven. Columns were also places of sacrifice and devotions. The flowering capitals of Corinthian order columns were, in myth at least, supposed to be inspired by an offering of fruit and flowers in a basket left atop a shaft in the fields, where foliage grew around it. If that overgrowth represented fecundity and fertility, that was no accident. The column is not just a symbol of man but also a symbol of the part that makes man a man. The male equivalent of the caryatid was the herm, a pillar crowned with a male sculpted head and often adorned with an erection. The word derives from Hermes, the god of fertility. Unlike caryatids, herms were free-standing, set on square bases and placed at crossroads, along borders and at critical points. They were symbolic structure made human, a union of the stone block and the organ of the intellect and the soul, the human head. The Romans adapted herms into more conventional sculptures with torsos and less prominent phalluses. The herm was transformed into the Terminus, named after the god of boundaries and landmarks. These were taken very seriously. The mapping of territory, the edge, was critical to the Roman sense of propriety – the unauthorized removal or vandalism of a milestone was punishable by death.

During the Renaissance these herms and termini were often attached as decorative elements to walls, diluting their purpose as markers. They have survived in contemporary settings as busts on brackets – see Sir John Soane's House for exactly how.

Mannerist architects in the sixteenth century and their acolytes in the nineteenth century also adopted this co-mingling of human and structure in the hybrid of an Atlas-like figure straining to hold up a structural corbel or bracket. Atlas was forced by the gods to support the heavens on his shoulders (occasionally he is depicted as holding up the earth itself). The Romans too had these figures, knowing them as 'telemons', named after one of Jason's Argonauts. Usually bearded, always with a naked torso, these figures make explicit the forces involved in structure by expressing them in human (if god-like) terms. That is, in effect, what columns, pilaster and pillars do. They are not only pivotal pieces of structure but they humanize building by making the forces legible at a scale we can comprehend.

34 PIPES, WIRES & SEWERS

THE ANTHROPOMORPHIC MODEL works well for parts of the house, with a façade as a face, a kitchen as a heart, a structure as a skeleton and so on. But nowhere is it more apposite than in the spaces behind the walls and floors, above the ceilings and under the ground as they increasingly fill up with a viscera of wires and cables, pipes, conduits and drains. The contemporary house is kept buzzing by an extraordinary tangle of hard wiring, copper piping, plastic tubes and, increasingly, by strangely intangible wireless networks, no more visible but just as important as the electrical connections of the synapses in the brain.

Terry Gilliam, in his magnificently dystopian view of a not-too-distant future *Brazil* (1985) conceived an interior landscape of fearsome technological incomprehension. Tiny, constricted apartments are squeezed between walls heaving with ducts, pipes and wires. The smallest technical problem leads to a complete collapse in the total environment – everything is reliant on technology. When our hero's air conditioning breaks down he falls asleep with his head in the fridge. In Gilliam's world the plumber is king. The saviour is, possibly uniquely, a guerrilla plumber (Robert de Niro in by far his oddest role) who turns up special-forces style, balaclava-clad to fix the bulging, heaving ductwork. It is the most brilliant contemporary parody of a fear of powerlessness against the failure of a technology on which we have become completely reliant, but more than that it suggests that our impotence in the face of a technology we have no control over perfectly parallels our impotence as actors on a bigger stage. Against an all-powerful, Kafkaesque state of endless surveillance and massive incompetence, resistance is futile.

But, of course, there is nothing new about pipes. The Romans had sophisticated plumbing and the sewage systems to take waste away, and they had under-floor heating and wooden water-supply pipes. But gas, which was brought into the house and piped into rooms in the nineteenth century, did represent a radical departure. Here was an alien material, a noxious but invisible gas introduced into living spaces to be burnt. It was a kind of magical alchemy. Of course it constituted a massive change in the night time scene, no longer bounded by the weak glow of candles, the evening could be extended at leisure in brilliant light. Then, after 1880, electricity, even less tangible, not even a substance at all, arrived. Suddenly the household could become a place of machines, vacuum cleaners, washing machines, fans, dumb-waiters, bells – all the things that had once consumed massive human energy could now be started at the flick of a switch. This panoply of consumer goods became, and remains, one of the key drivers to industrialization – there is just so much of it from mixers and juicers to TVs and fridges. Electricity has become one of the major building blocks of contemporary architecture. Yet there is no revelling in its presence, no celebration of the wires and conduits, fuseboxes and switches. Instead these are buried and concealed, hidden away, made invisible like electricity itself. For a moment, in the 1960s, ducts and cables, services and pipes were given their

179

due when a group of (mostly English) radical architects applied them to the building's exterior, brandished them like medals, attempted to put them where they could be easily changed and serviced. The moment reached its apogee with Richard Rogers and Renzo Piano's Centre Pompidou in Paris (Rogers was depicted on a satirical puppet show as having his guts spilling out as he talked) but fizzled out and was never, with any real conviction, applied to houses.

But Rogers had been hugely influenced by a very odd house in Paris designed by Pierre Chareau and Bernard Bijvoet, the Maison de Verre. Built for a gynaecologist between 1928 and 1932 in the courtyard of a Paris house, this glass block clad structure revelled in its revelation of pipes and mechanisms, exposing its veins and arteries like a dissected corpse. Everything is exposed, everything is visible, the copper pipes, the locks in the doors, the electric cable conduits and the very structure. It was a version of an ascetic, functional Modernism which revelled in its honesty and it chimed with a new idea of a healthy house, one in which dusty corners were eliminated, in which things weren't 'boxed in' but left in the light. It was a response to a Freudian fear of darkness, dust, of unknown, unknowable spaces, the unconscious bits of a dwelling.

The pipes and ducts, wires and cables kept coming. Phone lines, TV cables, air-conditioning ducts, pumps, boilers, radiators – it can seem as if there's barely any room left for structure. But these conduits are in fact every bit as much a part the structure of our daily lives as are the physical, load-bearing members of the house. Quite how critical a life support-system they are can be seen (as ever) in film. In any horror film there will be a moment when the power goes off unexpectedly. It is the accepted sign for trouble on the way. Likewise any thriller in which bad guys come to visit will be presaged by someone noticing that the phone-lines have been cut. This is the umbilical cut; bad things, we now know, will happen. In fact the very appearance of wires is bad. In Florian Henckel von Donnersmarck's *The Lives of Others* (2006) the protagonist tears his beautiful apartment's interior to pieces as he strips out the wires he finds, and he realizes that every intimate moment of his life has been recorded by the Stasi. The ripped-out wires leave a web of scars in the walls, visceral tracks to remind him of a tragic life.

British houses also find themselves in the rather unique situation of having their piping viscera exposed. In most countries, waste pipes, drain pipes, soil pipes, overflows and all the other endless tubes are buried in the depth of the wall (or occasionally they just run right through the apartments). In Britain they tend to gather like ivy on the rear walls so that if you look out of the window of a typical Victorian terrace or an Edwardian mansion block or chambers you will see an extraordinary web of black-painted pipes and hoppers, jutting overflows and rainwater down pipes. England's (once) incessant rain has been channelled into an architectural expression, a complex circuit diagram of water flow which is often so ugly that it becomes quite beautiful, creating a distinct back-yard landscape of black horizontals and verticals like a Mondrian frame.

More recently our floors have been filled with the rubbery hoses of underfloor heating (it took us two millennia to catch up with the Romans) and our TV and stereo cabinets have filled with incomprehensible spaghetti of cables. At the same time satellites on our roofs create a literal connection with the cosmos, receiving rays from satellites in outer space: an absolutely extraordinary idea yet one perhaps commensurate with the dominance of the TV screen in our rooms as a surrogate window to the world.

AFTERWORD: TIME, GHOSTS & THE UNCANNY

I WAS SPEAKING TO AN AMERICAN recently who had never lived in a house that wasn't brand new. To English ears, that sounds a strange idea, our housing stock is so old that we have become inured to the age of a home. In fact age has come to confer a certain value. At the top of the market old houses are desirable. This, however, does not stop the obsession with knocking through rooms, for adding kitchen extensions and conservatories, piling on loft extensions and digging out cellars as well as adding in endless en suites, which has made the historic skeletons of many of our historic homes almost unrecognisable.

Yet most of those homes have accommodated other lives before our own. They have witnessed dramas and joys, suffered the vagaries of interior fashions and have seen children grow up and perhaps people die. They will have sheltered myriad indelible memories and formative moments. Time is a critical element in even new homes, the accumulated marks of use, the thickening coats of paint, the slow deterioration of materials and components begins immediately a place becomes inhabited. There is settlement as houses find a comfortable position on the earth. The timbers dry out and crack, they deflect and bend. Floorboards begin to creak and crack, gaps open up, finishes and surfaces begin to mark and scratch, handrails and knobs begin to accumulate oil from many hands. And so time and the patterns of wear inscribe themselves into the fabric of the home.

I worked for a while at English Heritage while I was training to be an architect, and one of my jobs there entailed the analysis of paint in historic buildings, trying to discover what colours rooms, doors and mouldings had been painted at various stages of their existence. In taking a chip of a wall or a door you were able literally to peel back the myriad layers of history and taste. Colours would change from Queen Anne creams to Georgian greens through Victorian browns and maroons and nicotine stained beiges right up to garish seventies oranges and yellows and the neutral, tasteful off-whites of our own timid age. Each was separated from the other by layers of undercoats and strata of accumulated dirt, the cross section under a microscope appearing as a rainbow history of fashion.

Houses bear the traces of the events and even perhaps the atmospheres that existed within them. If this sounds a bit eccentric, think of the miasmas of smoke from fires (both hearth and house), pipes and cigarettes, think of the odours from food – every home has a distinctive smell which we recognize when we visit – though we are probably impervious to that of our own. Or think of the damp and mouldy smells of neglected or derelict interiors, or of mothballs or curries. All these scents are absorbed into the walls along with the steam from cooking and the endless exhalations and emanations from the bodies which had inhabited the spaces. This is why we redecorate when we move into a new place, in an attempt to mask the traces of previous lives.

Yet at the same time we are in love with historic homes. Britain in particular, with its peculiar blend of class snobbery – in which the new is traditionally disdained and wealth is inherited along with taste, possessions and homes and its nostalgic view of itself – puts a premium on age. It is as if a home needs to prove itself by having been around a bit and having survived. Of course the real reason is that in a densely inhabited land like Britain the best sites are all already taken and a rigid system of protection for historic buildings as well as for the countryside ensures supply of new houses is severely limited. The US has its own equivalent in the old established colonial era towns of the eastern seaboard, as do the grand Second Empire apartment buildings at the hearts of French cities.

But the question that most intrigues me is whether a house can retain emotional as well as physical atmospheres. Can intense psychic moments be captured in the fabric, just as smoke and smells are layered through the walls and floors – an archaeology of sensual inhabitation? We have all been into homes where we have sensed an 'atmosphere', something sinister or unpleasant, just as we have all had moments of clarity about places that just feel right – sunny, bright and sympathetic. Ghost hunters never find anything more than the most spurious evidence of hauntings, but they do quite frequently record huge differences in temperature between adjacent rooms, which are otherwise unaccountable for. Perhaps it is peoples' reactions to these which quite literally sends a shiver down their spine or makes the hair on the backs of their necks stand up – that odd feeling of being in a room that suddenly makes you uncomfortable.

Beyond a change in temperature, or the move from light to dark, beyond damp or decay, what is that causes these sensations? Is it nothing more than a series of preconceptions about the dark, the cold and the old, or is it a sense that dwells within us which can pick up the vibrations of the past? Of course, once we know that a house is supposed to be haunted, or that it has local superstitions and myths hanging around it, we are already unsettled, vulnerable.

Sites of evil deeds are often demolished, purportedly to stop them becoming ghoulish tourist destinations. The house of Fred and Rosemary West in Gloucester, scene of horrible murders, and another in Soham which became synonymous with the murder of two local girls, were both discreetly demolished. Rillington Place in London, notorious as the street where murderer John Christie lived at number 10, was renamed in an effort to expunge the ghosts of the past – though the house itself wasn't demolished until a road was built through it years later. These are all banal homes with nothing to distinguish them except a horrible history; they are not repellent, ugly or sinister in their own right.

There is no duty of disclosure about tragedies that may have taken place in a home, yet when buyers find out they are often shocked and if news leaks the home might prove impossible to sell. Corpses left to decompose on the floor leave a mark, staining the floorboards with their leaking fluids, and body parts may be buried in gardens, beneath cellars or in sewers. But this unease is not so much about the physical remains or traces – which will have been removed in investigations, but about discomfort with a history of trauma.

The haunted house is the idea that embodies the implications of this unsettling notion of emotional disturbance. The home is the most familiar of places, the symbol of family and domesticity of comfort and custom, so any disturbance to that sense of safety is felt far more keenly than it would be elsewhere. It is in this way that the haunted house becomes a symbol of angst or despair in other parts of a life. If ghosts are at the rather hysterical end of the spectrum, there is also an equally strange yet less fantastic sense of discomfort which emerges from what is known as the 'uncanny'.

The comedian Steven Wright used to do a routine about how he'd dreamt that everything in his house had been stolen and replaced with an exact replica. Then he'd woken up to find it was true. Just as in Shakespeare, the fool has the best lines. Wright touches upon a profound aspect of the domestic interior, a sense of the uncanny.

We identify so closely with our homes. They are so personal, so familiar and our relationship with them so intimate, that they become projections of ourselves, and any interference with them becomes unnerving and profoundly unsettling. It is almost a cliché to say on being burgled that it feels like being raped, but the very frequency of the analogy demonstrates the nature of our relationship with the interior. The English word 'uncanny' is rather unsatisfactory, far better is its German equivalent *das Unheimliche*, which translates as 'unhomely'. The word was popularized by German psychiatrist Ernst Jensch in his 1906 essay 'On the Psychology of the Uncanny', and he explains how the concept might be used in a novel in the creation of a character who is an automaton but whose status in never made entirely clear – an almost perfect encapsulation of the enduring appeal of *Blade Runner*.

But it was Freud who developed the theme further in his description of the uncanny as that which is strangely familiar, or familiar but strange. The architectural historian Anthony Vidler suggests that the uncanny is a symptom of the urban alienation engendered by the explosion of city life in the nineteenth century, through a rapid industrialization and urbanization. The walled town, formerly an intimate place in which residents knew their neighbours and the territory was familiar and based around a few key institutions had given way to a vast, unknowable city of recent migrants and unexpected events. In that case the house, the last refuge of the familiar in the tumult of the city, becomes a quasi-sacred place, and its disturbance, whether by ghosts, dreams, nightmares or intrusion, becomes a truly traumatic event.

The rich, strange and old world of symbolism embedded in our homes can be as unsettling as it is comforting. From the remnants of sacrifice and charms against witchcraft to our persistent efforts to stave off the effects of time and decay on the fabric of our homes, attempting to allay the processes we see at work on our own bodies at least in the finishes of our houses, their fabric is redolent with the ghosts and memories of an entire civilization. That we occasionally feel a shiver of something that has seemed to come to us without warning from the past is hardly surprising. The walls of our homes contain the ghosts of all those who have preceded us, memories of what was and yearning for what might have been.

BIBLIOGRAPHY

Adiga, Aravind *Last Man in Tower* (Knopf, 2011)

Alexander, Christopher *A Pattern Language* (Oxford University Press, 1977)

Bachelard, Gaston *The Poetics of Space* (The Orion Press, 1964)

Brunskill, R.W. *Vernacular Architecture: An Illustrated History* (Faber & Faber, 1971)

Cirlot, J.E. *A Dictionary of Symbols* (Routledge & Kegan Paul, 1962)

Cohen, Deborah *Household Gods: The British and Their Possessions* (Yale University Press, 2006)

Cook, Roger *The Tree of Life: Image for the Cosmos* (Thames & Hudson, 1974)

Denison, Edward and Yu Ren, Guang *The Life of the British Home: An Architectural History* (Wiley, 2012)

Eliade, Mircea *The Sacred and the Profane* (Harcourt, 1959)

Etlin, Richard A. *Symbolic Space: French Enlightenment Architecture and its Legacy* (University of Chicago Press, 1994)

Haining, Peter *Superstitions* (Sidgwick & Jackson, 1979)

Hersey, George *The Lost Meaning of Classical Architecture: Speculations on Ornament from Vitruvius to Venturi* (MIT Press, 1988)

Jankovics, Marcell *Book of the Sun* (Center for Hungarian Studies & Publications Inc., 2001)

Lanchester, John *Capital* (Faber & Faber, 2012)

Manguel, Alberto *The Library at Night* (Yale University Press, 2006)

Marc, Olivier *Psychology of the House* (Thames & Hudson, 1977)

Oliver, Paul, *Dwellings* (Phaidon, 2003)

_____, *The Encyclopaedia of Vernacular Architecture of the World* (Cambridge University Press, 1977)

Palasmaa, Juhani *The Eyes of the Skin: Architecture and the Senses* (Academy Editions, 1996)

Perec, George *Species of Spaces and Other Pieces* (Penguin, 1997)

Pollan, Michael *A Place of My Own: The Education of an Amateur Builder* (Bloomsbury, 1997)

Praz, Mario *An Illustrated History of Interior Decoration from Pompeii to Art Nouveau* (Thames & Hudson, 1964)

Rasmussen, Steen Eiler *Experiencing Architecture* (Chapman & Hall, 1959)

Rice, Charles *The Emergence of the Interior: Architecture, Modernity, Domesticity* (Routledge, 2007)

Rivers, Tony; Cruickshank, Dan; Darley, Gillian; Pawley, Martin *The Name of the Room: A History of the British House & Home* (BBC Books, 1992)

Rykwert, Joseph *On Adam's House in Paradise: The Idea of the Primitive Hut in Architectural History* (Museum of Modern Art, New York, 1972)

Sale, Charles *The Specialist* (Putnam & Company, 1930)

Saumarez Smith, Charles *The Rise of Design: Design and the Domestic Interior in Eighteenth Century England* (Pimlico, 2000)

Stevens, Anthony *Ariadne's Clue: A Guide to the Symbols of Humankind* (Allen Lane, 1998)

Tristram, Philippa *Living Space – in fact and fiction* (Routledge, 1989)

Venturi, Robert; Scott-Brown, Denise; Izenour, Steven *Learning from Las Vegas* (MIT, 1972)

Vidler, Anthony *The Architectural Uncanny* (MIT, 1992)

Vitruvius *The Ten Books on Architecture* (Dover, 1960)

Wiles, Will *The Care of Wooden Floors* (Harper Collins, 2012)

INDEX